CITY BOY

Praise for Mike Tedesco

"Politics and planning are intertwined, and politics is often rough and tumble. Thus, planners frequently fall into the fray. Political behavior can initiate from elected officials, from administrative personnel working for the elected officials, or from private interests seeking to manipulate them. Tedesco tells a story of a planner confronting the rough and tumble world of implementing plans. The story is earthy and raw. It is not an academic study, but a story told from the trenches. It is also a painfully accurate account of how good planning does not win based upon its merits. Entrenched interests, both inside and outside of government, will fight good planning to protect their positions through a variety of means, both legitimate and illegitimate. Implementing good planning takes long, hard slogging through endless battles. This is a story that too many practicing planners will recognize, and many who seek to become planners should come to understand before entering the profession."

—Kirk McClure, Professor
Graduate Program in Urban Planning, University of Kansas

"Mike Tedesco might well be the ghost of gonzo journalist Hunter S. Thompson returned to tell us what the life of a planner is really like, painting pictures embedded in a real-world reality that is too often ignored, or sanitized in academic planning textbooks. He uniquely combines planning theory with personal history. Tedesco provides with sharp clear insightful prose, sparing no one, including himself, a hard-hitting analysis of what an "innocent" new planner, as he recently was, may have to face, showing how and why we too often end up with ugly places and 'junk' landscapes. This book should be required reading in all planning schools. Don't wait for the movie. Read it now!"

—Gundars Rudzitis, Professor of Geography, Environmental Science, and American Studies; Adjunct Professor of Philosophy
Department of Geography, University of Idaho

CITY BOY

Urban Planning, Municipal Politics, and
Guerrilla Warfare

Mike Tedesco

SUNSTONE
PRESS

SANTA FE

Sunstone books may be purchased for educational, business, or sales promotional use. For information please write: Special Markets Department, Sunstone Press, P.O. Box 2321, Santa Fe, New Mexico 87504-2321.

Book design • Vicki Ahl
Body typeface • Bernard Modern Std
Printed on acid free paper

Library of Congress Cataloging-in-Publication Data

Tedesco, Mike, 1978-
  City boy : urban planning, municipal politics, and guerrilla warfare / by Mike Tedesco.
      p. cm.
  ISBN 978-0-86534-726-7 (softcover : alk. paper)
    1. City planning--Colorado. 2. Municipal government--Colorado. 3. Local government--Colorado. 4. Resort development--Colorado. 5. Community development, Urban--Colorado. 6. Environmental protection--Colorado. 7. Colorado--Environmental conditions. 8. Colorado--Social conditions. I. Title.
  HT167.5.C6.T53 2009
  307.1'21609788--dc22
                          2009023609

WWW.SUNSTONEPRESS.COM
SUNSTONE PRESS / POST OFFICE BOX 2321 / SANTA FE, NM 87504-2321 /USA
(505) 988-4418 / ORDERS ONLY (800) 243-5644 / FAX (505) 988-1025

To Caitlin

A trophy wife by any definition.

Contents

Preface

The names in this story have changed to protect its participants. To the largest scale possible, geographic place names have changed, such as the name of the town that provides the setting for this story, which presented somewhat of a challenge when citing local periodicals.

The following account is true and is based on real events. Alas, how does one cope with a constant barrage of incompetence? It molests your mind, your consciousness. Assailing you from multiple sources, multiple offenders, to the point where your defenses can't withstand the assault. As you beat one surge back another comes at you from behind, sideways. It creeps like a cancer, predictable, until one day you succumb.

Nonetheless, you keep fighting, because fight is the only thing you have left. If us planners are not carrying the fire, then who will?

1

Networking

Feet up, wishing I could light a smoke. Nothing like getting your fix at 8,200 feet. The air is thin in the mountains, but strangely, that never got to me. It was more the local population that gave me the headaches.

"I wouldn't worry so much about him," she said to the person on the other end of the phone, knowing full well I was in the next office. "People like him come to town, think they can change the world, and once they figure out they can't, they leave."

I should have been reading the fine print of the subdivision agreement sitting on my desk. Instead I tried, once again, to figure out what to do with the Town Clerk, Ava Mathews, my nemesis.

Politically, the place is a meat-grinder. Not because I was surrounded by a group of savvy individuals, more just by incident and induced by a healthy dose of incompetence. Like a sea-going salmon who has been thrown into a small pond full of minnows, knowledge of the wider world is moot if one can't master the discourse set by the dominant species.

What do I do? Go into her office and lay down the law? Suggest that her worldview merits a hearty laugh; that her lack of control over me has led to her current inferiority complex; that her 1986 hair style is a testament to her total lack of contact with reality? Such an approach might work—nothing else has. I have an uncanny talent when it comes to coping with people who are looking to pick a fight with me—it usually involves getting my ass kicked. On my 21st birthday, my brother, Paul, and I were waiting in line at a popular lesbian bar and I announced to everyone that the place was lame and we were leaving. Questioning the merits of everyone else's resolve to enter the drinking establishment insulted a group of five young gentlemen.

I took the big one, Paul the other four.

I knew it was our fight to lose, which is why I was a bit confused when the paramedics woke us up. Hmm, no blood. Clearly, the fight worked out well for me, but why was Paul bleeding? "What's the date today, son?" Looking around, nothing but the glare of flashlights. "What's the date today, son?" I spot Paul. He could see the question marks in my eyes, "It's your birthday," he yelled through the gauze pads. Indeed, he's right! "It's my birthday!" This impressed the health care and public safety professionals. They left. Paul and I got in the car and drove home.

"I don't know what's so special about his master's degree." She continued from her office. "It's not like urban planning is rocket science." Surely she must know I can hear every word of her conversation? "I don't know what he can offer that anyone else could not?" Rugged good looks, perhaps? "This town will never be an Aspen. Most of the time, he's out of the office, anyway, just being a little social butterfly." I've heard enough. Time to leave the office to see who's in the local coffee shop.

"Ava, I'm off to a meeting," I said toward the exit as I shot her a sideways glance.

"Wait," she responded with an urgency, signaling she disagreed with my judgment. "I need you here because I have to run some errands."

Why must she play these games? "Well, I can't help you out because I have some folks waiting for me." This, of course, was an absolute fabrication. But why should I be courteous enough to oblige her with honesty after listening to her conversation, poisoning the mind of who knows who? I left Town Hall and the cold air slapped the smirk off my face.

Maybe what troubled me most was that Ava was right. It's easy to be an urban planner—and it's easy to prove us wrong. Urban planning is to a professional field as reality TV is to reality. Grasping at straws for credibility, a hollow vessel with no underlying dominant theory, it's pretty easy to be a planner, and it's pretty easy to prove us wrong. We're not so special, but certainly better than civil engineers and architects. So I guess that puts us planners at the third rung from the bottom. Good news is, the ladder does not have that many rungs.

Generally, planners have a pretty bad reputation among the public. Why? Mostly because we attempt to advance equality, which pretty much makes us professional socialists. But it goes further than that; we're the ones who are telling you that you can't build your garage because it would be within a setback. We're the ones who are telling you that you can't start your home business because you're not in a commercial district. We're the ones who are the bureaucrats. We're the ones who say "no." A sexy profession? Not really, unless you're the one who can take credit for designing Paris. However, the funny part is, our weakness is also our strength. It is because planning draws from other disciplines' theories—geography, sociology, law, engineering, architecture, environmental sciences, economics, statistics, etc.—that gives us license to don any hat we see fit in any given situation. Like leeches looking for a host, planners have the liberty to draw expertise from a given field as we might deem appropriate. That's what I thought at least. I was fresh out of school and my first urban planning job wasn't going so well.

Let me see if I can sort this mess out: she hates me, she talks behind my back, she subverts me, she does not respect me, and she tries to subjugate whatever power that I might otherwise have. They didn't teach me how to deal with this stuff back in graduate school.

La Blanca Gente is nestled in the Colorado mountains. With a stable year-round population of roughly 1,000, the town is, from an urban planning perspective, a total mess. The "town" is a hodge-podge of subdivisions and commercial development arranged with absolutely no rhyme or reason. A bastard step-child of its mother county for years, it's clear that few gave the settlement the tenderness necessary for it to grow into a well-rounded and dynamic organism.

The political environment is that of pro-growth, as to develop the tax base. Pro-growth, that is to say, with a taste of growth management, which is where Mr. Urban Planner comes into play. When they hired me, "they" as in the seven elected town officials, the thought was that a growth boom was on the horizon and somebody needed to be around to deal with it, shape it, make sense of it. Sensing, like a gazelle before the lions pounce, that the predators are lurking somewhere unseen, the La Blanca Gente Town Board launched a preemptive strike against all those who wish to delve into the local real estate market. As far as I was concerned, hiring me was the best decision they ever made.

They were right, the town is ripe for a growth boom. As a pre-pubescent teenager is to *Playboy Magazine*, La Blanca Gente is to Colorado mountain resort towns. Not even close to being built out, hundreds of acres of raw land parcels await development and/or subdividing. More or less in the mountains, sitting on a bench at 8,200 feet, it is only a matter of time before the town is "discovered." Based on my employer's opinion of the situation, and my eagerness to line up a job after graduate school, I thought to myself, "This may well be the first step toward seating myself alongside the Gods of Urban Planning."

Excited as hell with two months to go before graduation, I really talked myself up, too. And with good reason. I was the only one of my peers who had landed a "Community Development Director" position. Most planning master's degree graduates start at the bottom. They get pigeon-holed into doing one mundane planning task or another, with very little wiggle room for professional development. Typically, it is the entry level planners who end up doing the run-of-the-mill code enforcement; i.e., zoning. In planning lingo, the term is not "zoning," it is "land use."

However you say it, though, it shakes down to the usual nonsense; they might-as-well just call it "government processing" because that's all they're doing. There's no difference between an entry level planner processing a public request than there is a cashier at the local driver's license bureau processing little Jimmy's very first license to drive. The only skill that is required for either position is patience. But me, the lucky bastard that I am, landed a gig where I may be able to actually do some good.

As far as the planning labor market goes, we're a dime a dozen. Supply is much greater than demand. Thus, when one finishes graduate school and enters the job market, one's value will only be in the neighborhood of $40,000 per year. Pennies, indeed, and it speaks to the lack of credibility planners have as a profession. In an attempt to boost planning's credibility, the American Planning Association (APA), which is likely the foremost professional organization for planners, offers what is called the "AICP" exam—the American Institute of Certified Planners. Like a CPA exam is to accountants, the AICP exam is to planners. The APA pushes their AICP exam like to take it is to take a drink from the Holy Grail. And, don't forget, that it costs $450 to take the exam,[1] another $195 for the official exam preparation guide,[2] passing the exam will raise your dues by about $100 per year,[3] and you'll have to pay for and attend 16 "certification maintenance" credits per year via seminars almost exclusively offered through the APA.[4] Indeed, AICP certification is a better revenue generator than credibility generator. Sadly, though, not only does a planner need a master's degree to have any prayer of getting ahead, one may be able to score some cheap credibility points with the AICP certificate hanging on their office wall.

In most cities and towns, however, AICP or not, planning master's degree or not, what you know is hardly relevant; it's how you play the local political game that counts. Because municipal and county employees are subject to the whims of elected officials, it's the planner's job to implement their decisions, however wrong they might be.

Urban planning educated planners hold the keys to the Promise Land. We're the only government employees that actually learned how to make cities and towns better. However, because the public administration educated city manager whispers into the ears of city council, because the law school educated municipal attorney whispers into the ear of the city manager, because the city finance director bemoans the cost of doing business, and because the public works director hammers at our credibility "because it wasn't planned by an engineer," is it any wonder that many cities and towns struggle?

When laymen are elected to guide the business and future of a municipality—a complex and dynamic organism—and such laymen are guided by trained bureaucrats (city managers), attorneys, accountants, and engineers, the answer to the question, "Why are there so many problems that face my city?" has just been explained. The contingent of professionals that should be the most leaned-on to steer policy decisions hardly have a seat at the table.

2

Aloha Means Goodbye

Brazen and cocky, it's the only way to fly. She came in through the front doors of Town Hall with an axe to grind. Not once since I started the job did she take the time to talk with me on a professional level other than a "hello" here and there. "Mike, we need to talk about last night," Tami said with a tone in her voice.

Smiling a big Tom Cruise smile, "Wow, it's been a while since a woman has said that to me." A twinge of guilt flickered in the back of my mind—don't put yourself in the position to get accused of sexual harassment, dip shit.

Clearly unmoved by my resistible charm, she started in on me: "You acted like a spoiled brat and I just want you to know that I don't appreciate the way you acted in front of the Town Board, particularly the way you acted toward Ava last night."

"I wasn't aware that you had a dog in the fight, Tami? But if you're looking to pick one with me, honey, I'm afraid you're way out of your league."

The La Blanca Gente Town Board would do well to fire Tami Inanis, their Marketing Director, mostly because no one is really sure what it is, exactly, that she does.

"Tami, what is it, exactly, that you do?" This is a good line of attack—always make the argument about them. "I've been here a couple of months and this is the first time that you've stepped foot into my office. I would have thought that we would be working a bit more closely—you being the town's Marketing Director, and I being the town's Community Development Director. There seems to be some missed opportunities here?"

Tami, perhaps at a loss for words (or not?) returned to the crux of her argument with me: "Mike, I just wanted to let you know that you acted like a spoiled brat last night."

"That's a theme of your argument that I understand, Tami, but it might help me to improve as your professional colleague if you elaborate on your point just a bit further?"

"You know what I'm talking about, Mike, and I just want to let you know that I think you acted like a spoiled little brat last night."

"Wow." I said as the smirk on my face grew, "You sure are persistent. If you are unwilling to engage me with constructive dialogue then very well. Thank you for your enlightening and positive comments. My door is always open should you feel motivated to express your opinions to me in the future."

She turned and strutted out the doors of Town Hall back to her refuge at the Visitors' Center. I sat for a moment somewhat confounded. Tami has now allied with Ava against me, and she lobbed the first volley of a cold war. She upped the ante by confronting me head-on. This may turn out to be a blood bath. Good thing La Blanca Gente only has, me included, four administrative employees. Not to worry, I can handle those two.

Now then, back to doing my fantasy football research.

The day of the move arrived—a typical sweltering late spring day in Lawrence, Kansas, the place I called home for the past two years. I was still recovering from my graduation party, which was celebrated perhaps a week earlier. The last thing I remember was pouring Sky Vodka into the fruit salad and sharing a nice picnic with a handful of my fellow graduates.

The Lawrence morning turned into midday, the humidity rising in conjunction with the temperature as if to mock me for physical exertion the day after a night on the town. Early June in Lawrence is pea soup. By supper time, the sweat pouring down my face, the truck was full and the house was clean enough to get our damage deposit back.

My wife, Caitlin, and I have been attending school since the day I accidentally got her pregnant and we subsequently moved in together. Thus marked the end of my partying days, and the beginning of my sporadic binge drinking days—both eras of my life I consider to be equally important. In high school, I was one of few kids endowed with the power to buy alcohol, partly due to my fast maturing Sicilian blood line, and partly because I got my hands on a fake ID, was I able to significantly contribute socially as a teenager. "Fake" in the sense that it was a valid ID, but the 22-year old gentleman pictured in it was not Papa Tedesco. Before I acquired the fake ID, I learned that if I took my shirt off before entering a convenience store, chances were, the cashier would sell me a pack of cigarettes without trifling me with questions of identification. By the magical time during my sophomore year when I acquired the fake ID, I was filling kegs and flirting with 30-year olds at local drinking establishments.

At Lewis and Clark High School in Spokane, Washington, popularity was measured by drug and alcohol tolerance, rather than more traditional qualities. Needless to say, I was pretty popular.

It took me seven years and a few million brain cells to get a master's degree, and for my wife, God bless her heart, five years to get her bachelor's. The day we emptied our house in Lawrence and closed the front door one last time, was the day we closed the door on the first chapter of our adult lives.

We drove off from our house, me driving the 26-foot U-Haul and my wife driving the 13-foot Mazda Protégé. Not yet ready to bid farewell to Lawrence, we make a B-line to my aunt and uncle's place for food and spirits. Besides my parents and perhaps a couple of stragglers that I have not considered, my aunt and uncle are two of the best people in the world. For two years, they kept my belly full of cabernet, India pale ale, and 5-star meals. As I see it, one day I need to return the favor. Needless to say, saying farewell to them was going to be a solemn occasion.

Ready, poised at the starting line, engines revving, all I wanted to do was make it to La Blanca Gente and start working. I had grown tired of academic life in graduate school. So much so that my patience was on pitiful display toward the end as I started peppering my writing assignments with foul language and punch-less editorials, of which my professors did not appreciate. Saying farewell to East Lawrence, the heart and soul of town, wasn't going to be easy, either. As far as low income neighborhoods go, and I've lived in them my entire life, East Lawrence is pretty sweet. Aside from the vagrants who were constantly walking through the neighborhood, I had no complaints.

We lived only a couple of blocks away from downtown. Brick streets, mature trees, dense foliage, old houses, alley ways, sidewalks, and a grid street pattern all add up to a great neighborhood. These days it's a grand hypocrisy and a cardinal sin for a planner not to utilize alternate forms of transportation. True to form, I tried to ride my mountain bike—the Cinder Cone—or walk as much as possible. Living in East Lawrence and only a couple of blocks away from downtown made it real simple for me to do so. There are few excuses I'll accept for planners to do otherwise. Many planners have a bad habit of not practicing what they plan.

The transition zone between downtown and East Lawrence is very subtle. If you travel east from downtown there are traditional commercial building fronts that pepper the streetscape. Old and dilapidated, many boarded-up, these buildings hug the sidewalks like a mother to child. Narrow, cracked like an aged face, the sidewalks have seen many souls.

Walking along these sidewalks, one is sheltered by matured deciduous trees, which provide definition and comfort for the pedestrian. East Lawrence and downtown Lawrence fade into or out of each other as if they are interlocking fingers. Urban planners would kill to design such a neighborhood. Alas, the tragedy is, East Lawrence is to Lawrence as Compton is to Los Angeles. No, the urban atrophic public prefers character-free subdivisions, with new pre-fab housing, where tree-lined streets, alleys, and sidewalks are meaningless.

All larger communities have their share of advocacy groups and Lawrence is no exception. Most of these people are simply misguided carpers that have too much time on their hands. Pluralism is a bitch and, as a public official, the constant barrage of sniveling is enough to make one hit the bottle. Be it planner, city council person, city manager, or whoever, the challenge of addressing special interest groups on a local level is that you're playing with nitroglycerin. Ignorance is bliss and facts mean little. Local advocacy groups have a bad habit of taking a position on an issue before all the facts are on the table. However, as public officials, much of the cross we bear is the time it takes to sit down and explain the reasoning behind our actions to local special interest groups. In the end, though, it's a lose-lose situation, because the same special interest groups that you take the time to sit down with and explain the facts and logic behind a decision making process will criticize you for taking too much time to make a decision regarding the same issue. Perhaps if planners and other public officials were to stop wasting our time sitting down with low credibility, high risk special interest groups justifying the decisions that we're making, the business of making your city a better place would happen much more efficiently? Then again, given the high degree of incompetence demonstrated on the local government level, perhaps these special interests groups are a good thing after all?

When I left East Lawrence, a five-story condominium building was nearly complete. Located on New Hampshire Street, perhaps, depending on your definition, adjacent to downtown. The East Lawrence Neighborhood Association (ELNA) was officially opposed to the development. Evidently, the folks in ELNA were not too happy with the height of the building. Now that it's complete, it is the second tallest non-KU building in Lawrence. Like most civic groups, misguided idealism drives the herd mentality more so than facts and logic. I don't think ELNA understands that the neighborhood of East Lawrence shares a symbiotic relationship with downtown. That is, what's good for downtown is good for East Lawrence and what's good for East Lawrence is good for downtown. The more wealthy people that live in this area, the longer the area will survive. I doubt this is the first phase of East Lawrence being gentrified. Worries about land values rising dramatically and, subsequently, squeezing the poor residents out are unfounded. A mixing of incomes is key to the continued vitality of neighborhoods. As it stands on the day I left East Lawrence, the only two income groups that were mixing are "Poverty Stricken" and "Homeless." Christ, even my wife and I were on food stamps.

Downtowns survive more because of the surrounding local populations that support them and less because of tourism and the WASP's driving in from the suburbs from time to time. Needless to say, placing high-end condominiums within walking distance of the bars, restaurants, coffee shops, and the whatever else of downtown Lawrence will help stem the tide of strip malls, cul-de-sacs, and general suburbanization that saps vitality from downtown and East Lawrence—the soul of town.

It's tragic, really, because propagandists from the City of Lawrence and the University of Kansas highlight downtown Lawrence as a place of charm and culture. Placing picturesque views of downtown and the surrounding neighborhoods in every brochure they can, the character of the area is a natural selling point to potential migrants. Both institutions, however, act as cancerous growths on the charm and culture of downtown Lawrence. The University of Kansas, an institution that adapts and changes at a glacial pace, is still designing campus expansion plans from a 1950s, modernist point of view—surrounding square brick buildings with parking lots and spacing them out with as much grass, landscaping, and surface parking as possible, which has created a college campus that is a real pain in the ass to navigate on foot.

For Lawrence's part, the city's Planning Department, guided by a horrifying land use policy, rubber stamps the strip malls, cul-de-sacs, and general suburban bullshit that saps potential consumers from the heart of the city. The travesty of the situation is that there is no planning in the Lawrence Planning Department; they need to skip the euphemism, and just call it the Lawrence Department of Institutionalized, Bureaucratic, non-Planning Code Enforcers. If ELNA had half a brain, they would be counting their lucky stars that a developer actually chose to develop in their neighborhood, because as it stands right now, East Lawrence and downtown could use the investment.

Thus were my rambling thoughts as Aunt and Uncle fed my family and gave us drink. After dinner, feeling just about right considering the cigarette I just smoked in the back yard, Uncle and I sat down in our usual fashion in the living room. A bottle of cabernet was nestled between my legs as I sat on the couch with a full glass in my hands.

My uncle, my dad's brother, is a man of fine Sicilian stock. A rambling talker with a PhD in Theatre and a long life full of trials behind him, his beard and hair now more grey than black, I always expect to listen more than I talk when it comes to conversations with him. His ridiculously sharp wit is the measure for which I judge others. Not to mention, his ability to look at a situation from all possible perspectives. For a Tedesco, a man is measured more for his ability to cut one down with intelligence than with brawn, which is a good thing considering my 135 pound, addicted to nicotine frame. That is to say, we're all smart-asses by nature; and my uncle is no exception.

Naturally, our conversation drifted into my plans for La Blanca Gente. I told him I was concerned about whatever good ole-boy political structure that I was either going to have to take down (assuming they're corrupt) or join (assuming they're not). He gave me his usual advice about taking it slow and being diplomatic. We joked about how "backwoods" La Blanca Gente is and how much of my future job will involve teaching and patience. After all, what the hell does La Blanca Gente know about planning? I had visions of dazzling the townsfolk with all the planning techniques learned from my time in academia, wining and dining developers over 18 holes of golf, steak dinners, and just generally being Mr. Metropolitan in a town full of folks who had never seen a real City-Boy.

The fantasies swirled through my head as the cabernet swirled through my veins. Keeping the subject of conversation on La Blanca Gente, my uncle massaged my clear excitement like a Thai hooker. When I graduated from the Department of Geography at the University of Idaho, I knew I was not yet ready to enter professional life, but now, only hours away from departure, I felt as sure as a Baptist on Sunday that I was the right man to take La Blanca Gente to the Promise Land.

It was roughly 9:00 in the evening, at this point, after a long day of loading the truck and cleaning, I was ready for bed. I stepped outside to smoke another smoke and take the last swill or two of my cabernet. I said a Novena to the Gods of Urban Planning and then bid farewell to my last humid, June Lawrence night.

I quickly drifted off into a cabernet induced sleep; my wife by my side. Awakening to the 5:00 AM alarm clock seemingly seconds after I closed my eyes, and facing a 10 hour drive to Denver in a 26-foot stick-shift U-Haul, I reluctantly got out of bed.

Eager to hit the highway and fulfill the day's prison sentence, we only stayed at my aunt and uncle's long enough for a quick shower and to grab a cup of coffee for the road. With twinges of emotion wondering where the last two years went, we exchanged farewells with the two people who nurtured our minds and bellies through graduate school, and we were off to Denver.

It only took a few minutes to grow accustomed to the hum of the U-Haul as I glided her down I-70. Wife and Daughter following just behind, I suspect they were as disappointed as I was to discover the beast I was driving had a governor at 65 miles per hour. The gentle rolling hills of east Kansas gradually leveled out to the High Plains of west Kansas, and the day grew warm. There's a wholesomeness that brews in west Kansas. While one side of my brain says, "what a wasteland," the other side says, "I could spend the rest of my life here." Perhaps it's because of the "Main Street" small towns whose best days are behind them, thus little change has occurred since the 1950s? Perhaps Kansas speaks to everyone's desire to pursue a simple life with a simple people? Or perhaps I'm just searching to justify the notion that Kansas would be a good place to pine the rest of my life away?

Such thoughts quickly fade as one crosses into Colorado from Kansas, however. The romance of the High Plains is lost in Colorado. Like trying to justify sex with an unattractive person, it's only natural for Kansans to attach virtue to their High Plains. Colorado, however, stimulates a love that is pure, like the moments after a first kiss, or looking at your newborn child for the first time. However, if you look closely, somewhere private and unnoticeable, she's hiding a putrid birthmark, like that thing on Mikhail Gorbachev's head only less obvious and even more ugly, and it's called the Eastern Plains of Colorado. Dusty, depressed, windy, dry, brown, run-down, run-out, and run-over, the virtue of the Colorado High Plains pales in comparison to that of Kansas, despite being nearly identical geographically.

Like a time warp, 10 hours later we landed in Denver. We spent the evening with my father, another man of fine Sicilian stock. He fed us steak and cabernet, at least that's what I had, courtesy of Mikey's Italian Bistro—the best Italian joint in the metro. Energized by the hustle and bustle of Denver, Dad and I split a bottle of wine and smoked a couple of cigarettes outside after Caitlin and Madelyn, my daughter of six years, drifted off to sleep. As I dripped the last drops of heavenly nectar into my wine glass from the bottle, I knew that sleep was approaching fast. I called my brother, Paul, to confirm that he would join us for the ride up to La Blanca Gente to help empty the truck, swallowed the last gulp of cabernet, and bid Father goodnight.

We left Denver at 6:30 the following morning to make our ascent into the Colorado High Country. Traveling up the Front Range in my 26 foot diesel powered Conestoga, Wife and Daughter trailing, and Brother with his daughter behind, we averaged about 35 miles per hour up the crest.

Once one starts the trip up the Front Range, the dry-land scrub of the High Plains quickly gives way to evergreen hills and dense wood-land. Like pioneers heading into the West, U.S Highway 285 was our wagon trail. Weaving south and west it took us, a winding trail that led us over 11,000 foot passes, high scrubland, and dry-land forests. The U-Haul groaned and moaned climbing the never-ending hills and navigating sharp mountain corners at 50 miles per hour. The clutch on The Beast was so stiff that I had to put all of my 135 pounds into it to shift gears; and down shifting into third gear, the highest gear I could stay in to get up the inclines, was like trying to fit a round peg into a square hole. With clouds of deep black smoke emanating from the exhaust, downshifting from fifth gear to third gear was a toss of the dice. On occasion, I would miss third and attempt to grind it into first gear. The Beast would snarl its teeth in dissatisfaction and reject my ignorance with opposing force. At times it was as if we were two heavy-weight boxers just feeling each other out, and times when it was like a scrum on the rugby field. Confusion reigned. Each incline would test my relationship with The Beast. The honeymoon of the High Plains was clearly over.

We stopped about half way up Poncha Pass to take a leak and sniff the air. We knew once we took the pass that we would make our descent into the San Luis Valley, the last leg of the trip and fine flat-land for The

Beast to travel upwards of its 65 miles per hour ceiling.

Functionally, that is to say, economically speaking, La Blanca Gente is considered part of the San Luis Valley. Rimmed by the Sangre de Cristo Mountains on one side, and the San Juan Mountains on the other, the San Luis Valley is sheltered from the warm winds that blow from Texas. The Valley, as locals call it, is also sheltered from the winds that blow culture and creative thinking from Denver, save for two state highways that manage to burrow new brain cells in from time to time. At roughly 7,500 feet, the Valley is a high desert with most of the rains coming during the monsoons of July and August. Potato farming and ranching are the predominant land uses. From a Euro-centric point of view, it's also the oldest part of the state; the Spanish Conquistadors came through some time back, slaughtered the natives, and claimed the land as their own. Culturally, the flavor of the Valley is still highly Hispanic, Native American, and Spanish.

Cold, dry, sparsely populated and highly isolated, the culture of the Valley is, also, insular. Change develops over the course of generations. Over my time in the Valley, I learned of grudges that still exist between pure-blood Spanish families and Native American families—grudges and bloodlines that have their roots in the days of the Conquistadors. History is long in the Valley. The Valley remembers. Stories passed through generations demand no documentation, just a patriarch to tell them. Names on a map may indicate settlement, but chances are it's a dusty one-road enclave consisting of perhaps a family or two that prefer to keep their ties private, and their business dealings beyond the gaze of gringo eyes; the faded old trailers and mobile homes, sagebrush yards, dust on the wind, blinding sun, rusted out old pick-up trucks—some run, some don't. Names on a map may suggest that there are places in the Valley that exist like other small towns in America exist—like other small towns with tree lined main streets and well kept green lawns overlooked by American flags flapping from front porches. In the Valley, one must shed their expectation of what small town America is because the Valley is more old-Mexico than gringo-defined and legislated Colorado.

Dayton Duncan tasted the Valley in his book, *Miles from Nowhere: Tales from America's Contemporary Frontier*. Duncan documents his travels exploring the American frontier—counties with population densities less than two persons per square mile, which is the metric the U.S. Census Bureau once formally used to define "frontier." Traveling through Saguache County, which encompasses roughly half of the San Luis Valley, Duncan explains that "Native Americans once considered the area a sacred and spiritual place where members of competing tribes could conduct vision quests in peace. Because of its powers, they called it the 'dream corridor.'"[5] The Valley that Duncan met in 1993 has changed little for the Tedescos of 2005.

Geographically, however, La Blanca Gente is more in the San Juan Mountains than it is in the San Luis Valley. In a narrow basin at 8,200 feet, the town is surrounded by ten to twelve thousand foot peaks. The hills surrounding town are able to suck enough moisture out of the sky to support dry-land timber—mostly Ponderosa Pines, but there are groves of Aspen and the occasional conifer or spruce. Just up the road from town is Wolf Creek Pass and the continental divide, a 10,500 foot obstacle that routinely receives more snow than any other pass in Colorado. The snow from the hills feeds the Rio Grande River, which is still a relatively insignificant stream of water as it passes through La Blanca Gente.

When I was 18 and still more interested in recreational drugs than aspects of life that are perhaps more important, a lady-friend and I crossed over the Rio Grande into Matamoros, Mexico, to find a good time. Up until now such a crossing represents my brief relationship with the Rio Grande. At this point in its journey from the snow melt of La Blanca Gente and the San Juan's, the Rio Grande is a muddied sludge puddle, incapable of supporting life that's higher up the evolutionary line than bacteria. The south Texas Rio Grande is a tired scrub-woman—used strictly for utilitarian purposes and ignored for the feminine virtues she once maintained. Drops of San Juan snow melt naively find their way into the Rio Grande, unaware of the life of servitude that lay before them. As it bisects Matamoros and Brownsville, the Rio Grande is only a ghost of its former self. In La Blanca Gente, however, the Rio Grande is still clear and cold, the virtues of which attract tourists from Texas, mostly because they had already fucked up their portion of it.

I wonder what my wife, following impatiently behind The Beast, thought of La Blanca Gente as we arrived in town. I got to see the place in March for my second interview. Caitlin, however, was not so lucky. I'll be frank with ya: La Blanca Gente is a terrible place—from an urban design standpoint, anyway. Never platted out like a traditional town, La Blanca Gente has suffered from years of nascent neglect at the hands of its mother county and the Colorado Department of Transportation. La Blanca Gente is a hodge-podge of buildings and streets that aggregate to absolutely no rhyme or reason. Like a puzzle scattered across the kitchen floor, all the pieces are floating around, but the town is as disjointed as towns come. Back in March when I came through for my second interview, the town fathers insisted they needed someone to manage the growth and to help put the pieces together. They were like cold and hungry orphan children begging for someone to take care of them. I, still staring at the specter of unemployment after graduate school, was hungry myself, so it appeared that the burgeoning relationship would work well for both parties.

We pulled into our rental home—surrounded on three sides by undeveloped, sagebrush covered lots—and started the arduous chore of lifting heavy objects with minds, bodies, and white blood cells still accustomed to the near sea-level of Lawrence, Kansas. Paul's daughter— my niece—and my daughter, managed to keep themselves busy playing around the brown dirt patch that was once a grassy front yard.

Naturally, Paul and I did most of the heavy lifting while my wife directed traffic. The first day we spent in La Blanca Gente was fairly warm—pushing 80 degrees. The thin dry air is not very conducive to breaking a hard sweat like a humid 80 degrees in Lawrence, but Paul and I did our best. We decided to take a break, puff down a smoke, and adjourn to the local liquor store to pick up some cold ones. We made our way down Colorado State Highway 2—Heaven's Highway—which forks off of U.S. Highway 1 right in the center of town. Like a shark that can sense a potential meal from up to a mile away, Paul and I instinctively found the nearest liquor store without any problem. We picked up a sixer of IPA's, another of Corona, and stopped into the neighboring gas station, which doubled as a Blimpies sub shop, for some sandwiches and a lime. After lunch we finished unloading The Beast and managed to return it that day. Paul and his daughter left that evening, to be met again soon on a golf course in Denver, no doubt.

I had one week to prepare for my first day on the job. With expectations running high and my anxiety building, this will be a job I know I will love. My positive thinking was massaged by the fact that there is no town manager, which means I don't have a direct boss; no job description, only a vague portrayal of town needs; a one-man "Planning Department," which means, so long as I have the blessing of the Town Board, I can do as I see fit; and, last but not least, only three other administrative employees, all of whom I share equal power with: the Chief of Police, the Marketing Director, and the Town Clerk. The town farms out their legal work to a firm located in a bigger city on the Valley floor. As I see it, the future is looking bright for La Blanca Gente.

I was somewhat worried about establishing relationships with the local real-estate developers seeing how I have a tendency to think of developers as greedy and conniving bastards; but I figure, so long as I remain as unbiased as possible, there shouldn't be too many confrontations. I was also worried about the good ole-boy network I was sure to confront. No doubt if they don't accept me, it'll be a problem. And what about my fellow colleagues? The Town Clerk seemed, from my experience with her at least, to be an old-hat at directing administrative traffic. The Marketing Director, however, I knew nothing about and was curious as to what it is, exactly, she does. The Chief of Police I had chatted with once or twice over the phone, and he seemed like a reasonable guy. All and all I didn't have a lot of worries.

A couple of weeks after my family and I had arrived in town, my father decided to come down from Denver to enjoy a weekend gallivanting with his son. A week earlier my wife and I had dropped $70 for an atrocious meal at what was supposed to be one of the finest restaurants in town. The damn place was charging $7 for a glass of house cabernet that one can purchase for $7 a bottle. With my dad around, I thought we would tempt our palates at the local golf club. After eating a mediocre Ausso Bucco and drinking three glasses of a delightful house cab, Pops and I decided to drop off the girls and hit the local drinking hole.

We pulled into a full parking lot that surrounds the saloon—always nice to see commuters having a few drinks on a Saturday night. We walked into the establishment to a band playing a cover of Van Morrison's "Brown-Eyed Girl." The near capacity crowd of roughly 150 people ate that shit up. I knew immediately that I was out of my element. In fact, I felt like I had just walked into the Double Deuce, the bar that Patrick Swayze bounced in the film *Road House*. I was surrounded by cowboys, too many damn cowboys. Dad and I might as well have walked into the gorilla exhibit at the San Diego Zoo. After "Brown-Eyed Girl" the band went into their set of country cover tunes, the names of which I care little to remember.

Glancing around the crowded venue I only noticed perhaps three or four people who appeared to reflect my definition of normal. Worse yet, the males outnumbered the females by about three to one. I couldn't help but get the feeling that if I got caught looking at a woman, some ego driven hick would try to pick a fight with me. Not to mention, the place was almost to the point of standing room only. I gotta admit, though, I was impressed by the locals' enthusiasm for having a good time. Such positive sentiments aside, I could smell a bar-fight in the air. It must be a male instinct, a result of testosterone; the room was overflowing with big male egos and my brain, triggered by a carnal sense, pumped messages to my body to be ready for anything. I sipped my beer as cautiously as a gazelle grazes grass on the Serengeti. I day-dream about slamming the bottle across the face of the first guy that attempts to give me a hard time, that or the first guy I pick a fight with. Being only a feather-weight means one has to be creative with the rules of engagement. Should some 230 pound brute pop an attitude in my direction, if I don't strike first with the cheapest of cheap shots, no doubt one punch would be enough to bring me down.

Controversy is my puppy—following me around always looking for attention. I try to ignore it as to go about my business undistracted, but it does not take long for me to give in and embrace it. Hopelessly searching for Patrick Swayze, I spotted Truett, one of the seven Town Board members—one of my seven bosses—and flagged him down to join us. At this point in the evening the pale ales were going down smooth and I had adopted a habit of chain smoking.

I introduced Truett to my dad and we started drinking in a ritualized fashion. Truett is young, perhaps my age, not even thirty. He's a local who only went away for a few years to earn a master's degree in business administration—gotta' admire that. He's also a fairly good looking young lad who tends to favor a cowboy way of seeing things, which is something I'm willing to overlook.

We talked as best we could with the bullshit band playing in the background. It's tough to carry a decent conversation with the decibel level so high, but we managed. He said what I expected him to say: "Ya, your position may well get political and you'll have to put up with some garbage, but I think you'll do just fine." Then, Truett said something that caught my attention: "Stay on Ava's good side; you really want to stay on Ava's good side."

Huh?

I had dealt with Ava during the hiring process and, although I could tell her personality wasn't really my brand of gin, I didn't expect to develop a negative relationship with her. After all, what business does the Town Clerk have with the Planning Department?

The three of us downed a few more pale ales. Truett was actually drinking Budweiser; needless to say, the lad could use some culture, and then Dad and I left for the comforts of home. My first of hopefully many nights out on the town wasn't bad, especially in the company of my father. I was somewhat worried, however. How long will it be before some hick tries to pick a fight with me? How long is it before I really get fed-up with the locals? How long will it take me to adjust? What happens if I don't like my job? And, why didn't that bar have an IPA on tap? Eventually, though, the worries faded away as I drifted into a deep, alcohol induced sleep.

3

Shelob

La Blanca Gente Town Hall, no bigger than a three bedroom, one story house, does not inspire much civic pride. Four days before the big date, with the new house nearly arranged and organized, I dropped by to unload some books and files I thought would come in handy during my tenure in La Blanca Gente.

I got the sense that Ava, the Town Clerk, felt a twinge of discomfort when I showed up with five boxes of books and three boxes of files filled with old journal articles, all a result of my college career. I went to graduate school because I was attracted to urban design. I left graduate school with a specialization in economic development. The marriage of sound urban design principles and the practice of financing and implementing real estate developments works out pretty well because, although I wholeheartedly agree with contemporary urban design theory, the primary proponents of such design push contemporary theory with more fervor and veiled virtue than Jerry Falwell. To make matters worse, most of these New Urbanist Evangelicals could recite a sermon to you that could make one feel eternally damned for buying that house on the fringe of town. However, what they can't do, and what they need to be able to do, is speak this language in real estate development lingo. That is, stop framing the argument in terms of virtue and start framing the argument in terms of profit potential. Instead of telling developers that if they develop "the right way," it's better for pedestrians and the welfare of planet Earth, planners should explain the matter in terms of internal rate of return on the developer's (or his investors') equity investment.

In order to speak the developer's language, however, a planner must understand it, as well, and this is precisely where the breakdown in education occurs. In municipal planning, this is the difference between being a simple-minded bureaucrat and an agent for change. Waging pitched battles against attorneys, engineers, and developers advocating for smart urban design is a frustrating position for a planner to take because, from the perspective of the developer sitting across the table, and from the perspective of the city manager and city council, planners are the one piece of the puzzle that stymie private profit potential and new tax revenues. When observing those who argue for virtuous urban planning, the ones who win the day frame their arguments in monetary terms. Virtue is just the icing on the cake.

The irony here is that, generally speaking, the battles that planners fight advocating for smart growth tend not to be with the development community but with colleagues on city staff, not the least of which being the city manager. It's not necessarily the development community that says "no" to New Urbanism. The only thing the development community wants from a municipality is a predictable set of guidelines for them to process their developments through, because predictability minimizes risk. If a planner can give them that, then you could require them to give you a nice foot rub so long as their subdivisions are granted an expedient municipal approval process.

Ava and I chatted outside for some time. The front door of Town Hall faced a big surface parking lot. When I say "big" I mean big enough to park a slue of RV's and other high-profile vehicles. During my tenure in La Blanca Gente, as I braved the wind and chill temperatures to feed my monkey, I often wondered if the parking lot was little more than an absurd waste of public space.

Town Hall actually fronted Highway 2. Travelers along the highway, however, have absolutely no clue what they are passing when they drive by it. The architecture inspires nothing to catch the eye, nothing that says, "Listen here you Texan, tourist, cock-sucker, you're in La Blanca Gente now and this is the building where the decisions are made." No, travelers can't even see the freakin' front door as they wiz by, because the front door does not open up to passers-by on the highway; it opens up to a surface parking lot. Next door to Town Hall is the Visitors' Center, which, at least, offers a gazebo and some landscaping surrounding it. Here is where you will find the woman responsible for letting the world know about La Blanca Gente: the Marketing Director. Indeed, queen of her own little fiefdom. I sat and stared at the Visitors' Center and pondered what it is, exactly, the Town of La Blanca Gente Marketing Director actually does.

Ava's long blond hair, short and pouffy bangs, high-waisted jeans, and a tee-shirt that hid her belly underneath a blouse that was hiked up just below her breasts, reminded me of Cindy Lauper videos I watched as a youth.

Ava grew up in Creede, Colorado, just up Highway 2 from La Blanca Gente. Creede is an old, busted mining town that is limping along and surviving on the tourist dollar. By all measures, Ava is a local. She started with La Blanca Gente soon after it incorporated in 1993. Armed with her high school diploma, Ava worked as a front desk receptionist in Town Hall. Outlasting everyone else by attrition or, perhaps, just a simple lack of ambition, she worked her way up to Town Clerk. Ava was open with the fact that she graduated high school and took a couple of college courses that amounted to little more than a waste of money. No, she learned on the job. Through her years of experience, Ava had developed a perception about public planning that would inevitably clash with my own. It appeared to me that, in Ava's mind, the town planner is the town code enforcer, which, depending on what town one is planning for, may be the case. The euphemism amongst professional planners for such a position is "current planning." Current planners do nothing more than react to whoever is walking through the doors of city hall wishing to develop whatever it is developers develop. Current planners are bound by municipal code adopted by city councils, one does not arbitrarily sway from the code, one simply must follow its direction.

It is difficult to argue that planners exercise planning techniques when practicing current planning. One certainly does not need to have an education to be a current planner. In fact, such words combined together—"current" and "planner"—create a paradoxical phrase, two opposing definitions attempting to work together as one, a yin and a yang. Like Newton's third law of motion, the equal and opposite reaction to planning is "current." Such a contradiction of terms does not boost the value of planning's credibility. Someone is going to have to talk with the American Planning Association about this.

As we sat outside on a warm La Blanca Gente afternoon, Ava suggested to me that the eight boxes worth of literature that were sitting in my car were unnecessary to bring into the office. "I don't know when you would need those books," she said, "but whatever."

Sensing from Ava's tone she did not appreciate me bringing the books into my office, I replied in a chipper tone: "I know, man, but I just can't get enough of Elizabeth Plater-Zyberk—she's dreamy."

"Huh?"

It appears I should skip the literary references with Ava, so I clarified: "I don't know when I'll need them, either. That's why I would prefer them in my office, so they're on hand in the event that I do need to consult one of them."

Ava's retort was quick: "None of the other Land Use Administrators needed books around."

I let out a breath of mild frustration and I replied, "Perhaps, unlike my predecessors, you'll find that I'm full of surprises." And, by the way, did she just call me a "Land Use Administrator?" I'm the Community Development Director, damnit.

I proceeded not to heed Ava's advice about the books and carried them into my office. My corner office, that is, which, despite the great views, was a freakin' mess from neglect and being a general staging post for all the documents Ava didn't know what the hell to do with. No matter, I'll deal with it soon enough. I noticed why Ava called me a "Land Use Administrator." It was the title on the plaque beside the doorway into my office. As one of my first matters of business, I'll have to get that changed. I left Town Hall with a nod to Garrett Cook, the Chief of Police, who, despite my overall suspicions of cops in general, I figure to be quite the stud.

I left Town Hall thinking, perhaps a bit sarcastically, that Ava is nothing but charm. When it occurred to me, as I opened the car door, that I would be spending as much time with Ava as I do with my wife, my sarcasm quickly turned to anxiety and the smirk that was on my face quickly whimpered away like a scared kitten. I tried to analyze the situation on the three minute drive home.

Getting home, kissing Daughter and Wife, then adjourning to the garage to feed the monkey with a glass of wine and cigarette or two, I pondered such a notion: "She learned on the job, so what does that mean for me?" Does it mean that all definitions of what La Blanca Gente town administrators are "supposed to be doing" are based on her flawed perceptions that stem from her experience in La Blanca Gente? Does it mean that the woman has grown professionally in a bubble and long ago that bubble veered off course from reality and what's left is the situation known as La Blanca Gente town administration? Is that a bad thing? Finally, and most importantly, the question that followed me to bed that evening was, "In the absence of knowledge, is there opportunity?"

Awakening the following morning, a notion was conceived in my mind that pumped an element of fear into my heart: "Maybe, by virtue of her longevity, Ava has outsmarted everyone." Worse yet, she called me the "Land Use Administrator." My predecessors were all un-trained planners, meant only to enforce the Town of La Blanca Gente Land Use Code. Un-trained, which means, at least during their time in La Blanca Gente, they didn't know shit. All they did, and there were two or three "planners" before I came around, was enforce the town's land use code. Once again, I return to the topic of "current planning" and how much that euphemism purely misses the mark of what planners ought to be doing. Planners don't follow directions; we make the directions for others to follow. Thus, from where I'm sitting, Ava's interpretation of planning is nothing more than code enforcement.

Perhaps to blame for Ava's perception, however, is not her educational level but more the field of planning itself. The problem is that most planners would have a hard time defining their field. It's a flimsy, ambiguous profession. The first books I read on the subject of cities were James Howard Kunstler's, *The Geography of Nowhere* and Andres Duany's et al., *Suburban Nation*. Up until that fateful semester of Urban Geography when I was a college junior, frankly, I wasn't even aware that the current suburban development status quo was even considered a problem. Ignorance is bliss, and I was not alone. The University of Idaho, in Moscow—a cozy small town on the rolling hills of the Palouse in northern Idaho—is fed by suburban kids from Boise pursuing college degrees who consider Moscow a welcome interlude before returning to Boise to pine away the rest of their lives. Boise, though it does have a healthy urban core, is the quintessential suburban city. The city was largely built during the growth years of the nineties and is the poster child for the "New West." As an aspiring planner, I would tell you that Boise has serious problems. But try telling that to the kids who grew up there. Like most people, they are just not aware of the pitfalls of suburban development. To them, it is all normal. For the generations who have grown up in the suburbs, and for those who aspire to buy a single family home at the end of a cul-de-sac, someone needs to be responsible for telling these people that their actions have consequences. Thus my first impression of planning was defined by Kunstler and Duany, two of planning's latter-day saints. Their definition of planning is driven by aspects of urban design, and thus is mine.

My old graduate school buddies and I often laugh at our perception (expectation?) of planning before we entered the labor market versus our perception of planning after we entered the labor market. Perhaps this applies to many people who quickly become confused and disenfranchised with their chosen profession quickly after entering the market. Planning has some potential. Trouble is, we're just un-cool. No Hollywood writers create films or television series based on the professional practice of a planner. No, no, because we're the girl with buck teeth, glasses, and we haven't washed our hair in a few weeks; just standing in the corner while the party happens all around us. We have our eyes on everyone, but no one so much as nods their head in our direction.

Urban planning is such a broad topic, one could define us just about any way one deems appropriate. The American Planning Association can't even narrow down a sturdy definition of the field. Is Ava wrong for calling me the "Land Use Administrator?" No. But all it means is that my sole responsibility, according to her, is to administer the land use code, i.e., be the bureaucrat. No discretion, no ambiguities. If someone walks in the door and needs some "planning," I turn not to my own expertise and creativity; I turn to the code, and if it says "no" then I say "no." Period.

Thus is the discourse within, tragically, most municipalities. Planners are not planning; we're just following directions. How the American Planning Association, in their infinite wisdom, let planners sink to such a level, is a question that must be addressed.

It's all so simple, really. During the industrial revolution and up until 1926, titans of capitalism showed little regard for the consequences of their real-estate decision making. Smelters and alike were placed adjacent to residential neighborhoods and belched whatever it is that smelters belch upon the masses. Or, to argue the point from a different perspective, residential neighborhoods sprung-up around the smelters to house the labor needed to make the world go-round. *The Jungle*, by Upton Sinclair, paints an accurate picture of the stockyard neighborhoods of early 20th-century Chicago. "There is over a square mile of space in the yards," wrote Sinclair, "and more than half of it occupied by cattle-pens; north, south, as far as the eye can reach, there stretches a sea of pens."[6] Needless to say, the neighbors must have grown increasingly upset by this.

As time drew forward, municipalities started to segregate the unhealthy but necessary industrial land uses from everything else, such as residential areas. The emerging trend came to a crescendo when planners for the Village of Euclid, Ohio, put the clamp down on Ambler Realty, which was looking for a wholesale free-pass to develop as they saw fit on a 68-acre tract within city limits. The Supreme Court upheld Euclid's decision to apply their zoning ordinance to Ambler Realty's development in an effort to steer the nature of it and, thereby, protect adjacent landowners. In his opinion, Justice Sutherland dreamed up a million-dollar simile likening the development to placing a barnyard animal indoors "like a pig in the parlor."[7] And thus zoning gained the case-law it needed to bloom into what is perhaps the primary driver of municipal bureaucracy today.

Two years prior to Euclid vs. Ambler, the U.S. Department of Commerce drafted the Standard Zoning Enabling Act, which, today, is still the standard template for state land use enabling legislation.[8] Between the Department of Commerce and Euclid vs. Ambler, the seeds of the American Planning Association's dyslexic fetish with "current planning" were sewn. Bent on finding ways to better regulate real estate development, the American Planning Association's veins pump with the ghosts of separating the smelters from everything else.

After World War II, zoning evolved rapidly to accommodate the automobile. First appearing in southern California, strip-malls bloomed throughout the country as the product of zoning regulations that required on-site parking. Thus was the death of "Main Street" forms of commercial development. The status quo of urban design no longer considers pedestrians on the sidewalk; it now considers automobiles on the street, and where to put those automobiles in the event they choose to park. Suburbs, decaying central business districts, malls, big box stores, strip-centers, traffic congestion, mazes and mazes of twisty-turny streets, all of which seem to end in a cul-de-sac, are all products of zoning (land use) codes that steer the real estate market to organize in the manner that it develops today.

New Urbanism, smart growth, traditional neighborhood develop-ment, or whatever you want to call it, represent the backlash toward such development patterns. Such philosophies place the pedestrian back as the priority "being" that will be served by new development, not the automo-bile. The important point to remember, however, is that the post World War II development pattern is guided by reams and reams of municipal zoning law, as is the case in La Blanca Gente. If La Blanca Gente were to build-out, the current zoning code would require such a build-out to look very much like every other suburb in every other city in America, with little distinction other than the mountains that frame the scene. Needless to say, James Howard Kunstler would be disappointed.

If Ava envisions me being the shepherd for such a scenario as the "Land Use Administrator" then our relationship is bound to disintegrate quite rapidly. A planner's role should not be that of bureaucrat; it should involve manipulating the market to fit whatever virtue we're trying to push at the time. Planning is great, because at its core, planners were meant to be "The Ideas Guy." But somehow, we've evolved to the role of a bitter, nagging wife—half neglected, but kept around out of necessity because hey, somebody's gotta' process those subdivision proposals. The only thing bureaucratic planners manipulate is the virtue of "current planning." As planners, we've accepted the fact that our roles are fairly minimal as "change agents." The goal of organizations like the American Planning Association is to extol the virtue of sound urban design via stringent municipal zoning codes. Virtue is meaningless unless one can show it generates a predictable monetary return.

Take, for example, New Urbanism, a virtuous philosophy, indeed. No doubt swaying away from traditional suburbanism and steering the urban design of developments toward a more traditional, pedestrian friendly approach is worth the effort. However, starting a local war in an effort to adopt it does not do planners any favors, nor does it add to our positive image. Money talks, and to a developer, adding risks (real or perceived) to his subdivision proposal is not the way to endear yourself to his heart. Next thing you know, the "business community"—developers, lenders, investors, engineers, real estate agents, title agents, contractors, etc.—are whispering poison in the ears of city council members, bad mouthing the city's land use policies. Now the city manager is panting down your neck passing the heat he's feeling from city council down to you, the planner, the instigator, the bad guy. You don't need that kind of headache and it certainly doesn't help your credibility.

The point is that planners spend a whole lot of time dreaming up good ideas, but we neglect to spend any time figuring out how those ideas can be situated into the marketplace. If you're a planner, like the American Planning Association taken as a whole, and you're pushing whatever it is that you push, the only people that are listening to you and accepting your arguments are your fellow planners. You're preaching to the choir.

Planners that are in the trenches of municipal planning need to be pulling levers at the same time they're pushing them. If we're adding money to a development proposal, we need to be subtracting money somewhere else. And therein lies the rub. Planners are pretty damn good at finding ways to add to the costs of a given development proposal, but we're pretty damn bad at finding ways to subtract from them. I can't imagine being a developer, sitting across the table from some punk who makes $50,000 a year, who is trying to add $500,000 in costs to my proposal. No wonder nobody likes us.

These days, many municipal zoning codes have more insidious motives than just simple zoning. Municipalities argue that it's in their citizens' best interest to regulate that all houses be constructed with gold bricks, because the silver bricks just don't have the same pizzazz. Simply put, leaders of small, suburban municipalities have figured out that in order to maintain the quality of living within their communities, the zoning code is the most reliable tool to employ. In such places zoning is not a matter of keeping the smelters away from the working class. No, it's a matter of keeping the working class away from their communities. Exclusionary zoning is a common practice in upper income suburban municipalities eager to keep the vagrants out and the wealthy in. That is to say, much of today's zoning practice is less to separate incompatible land uses and more to separate incompatible income levels.

There is some case law that has struck down the most blatant of exclusionary zoning. Mount Laurel, New Jersey, attempted to require minimum lot sizes and minimum square footage requirements to keep developers from producing affordable housing within their upper-income community. Like Zeus upon a mountain top, the Supreme Court struck down such requirements. Not far from Lawrence, Kansas, is the primo Kansas City suburb of Mission Hills, Kansas. Thomas Frank, in *What's the Matter with Kansas*, describes Mission Hills as ". . . a classic illustration of what elites are all about. Its two square miles of rolling, landscaped exquisiteness house a population of about thirty-six hundred with a median annual household income of $188,821, making it by far the richest town in Kansas and, indeed, one of the richest in the country."[9] How do you think places like Beverly Hills stay Beverly Hills? Indeed, the market plays a large part, but markets are not static—particularly real estate markets. No, municipalities like Beverly Hills and Mission Hills stay exclusive because their planners insure success is crystallized within the city land use codes, which is the best excuse to give excuses why one can't build developments that may cater to the under-class.

Sometimes municipal zoning codes don't go far enough. It's common knowledge that most new subdivisions will be controlled with property covenants in addition to municipal zoning law, i.e., a homeowners' association. Joel Garreau dubbed them "shadow governments" in his book, *Edge City*. As Garreau explains, "These shadow governments have powers far beyond those ever granted rulers in this country before. Not only can they prohibit the organization of everything from a synagogue to a Boy Scout troop; they can regulate the color of a person's living room curtains."[10] The irony is that upper income, white, churchgoing, pro-property rights zealots willfully sign away a vast majority of their property rights the instant they sign their mortgage. Clearly, in their minds, principles take a back seat to protecting one's property value. Developers don't even try to hide the fact that if you buy within their subdivision you'll have a hard time letting your dog out without the homeowners' association panting down your neck like a sex-starved teenager. In fact, developers have found homeowners' associations so successful that they use them as marketing tools.

I almost hate to take my argument a step deeper, but in this case, it's appropriate: in 1755, Jean-Jacques Rousseau published *Discourse on the Origin of Inequality* by which he argued, "The true founder of civil society was the first man who, having enclosed a piece of land, thought of saying, 'this is mine,' and came across people simple enough to believe him."[11] Rousseau continues by asking the question, "How many crimes, wars, murders, and how much misery and horror the human race might have been spared if someone . . . would have cried out, 'beware of listening to this charlatan. You are lost if you forget that the fruits of the Earth belong to all and that the Earth itself belongs to no one!'"[12] Daniel W. Bromley coined the term "Rousseau's revenge" when comparing the consequences of the Federal Endangered Species Act (and environmental legislation in general) to private property rights or, as Bromley phrases it, "the freehold estate."[13] Because, as Bromley puts it, "I reveal no great secret to suggest that the freehold estate is in a rather bad state. Just how serious is the threat can be assessed by the aggression of the many organizations whose sole purpose is to celebrate and protect private property."[14]

I would argue that Bromley's thesis can be extended to property rights activists—those that have a general indignation toward zoning and the concept that there is a place for government to determine what one can or cannot do with his private property—and those who willfully reside within subdivisions that enable homeowners' associations to dictate what is the best use of their property. With one hand they vote for anti-government republicans, and with the other they willfully agree to live in a neighborhood that is tantamount to a socialist enclave.

But let's set the history of zoning aside and just consider the merits of Euclidian zoning within La Blanca Gente and the fact that I'm the one responsible for enforcing it.

Give the man a high-five. Woo-hoo. I'm jumping out of my pants. If Ava, the Town Clerk, thinks that my primary job is enforcing La Blanca Gente's zoning code because I'm the "Land Use Administrator," the little boy inside of me, ya know, the creative kid who just wants to move to Paris and write poetry all day in some corner café and explore the multitudes of enrichment experimenting with recreational drugs, felt a twinge of anxiety after our exchange in Town Hall's parking lot. God forbid I take some literature into my office that actually attempts to explore what it is that urban planning is. Because, frankly, at this point, I'm a little confused, too.

Nonetheless, Tedesco the "Land Use Administrator" is also Tedesco the "Community Development Director"—a term that encompasses the many ambiguous facets of my being, a term that grants me the freedom to exercise my community development expertise in whichever direction I deem appropriate.

John Reps got it right when he said, "Zoning is seriously ill and its physicians—the planners—are mainly to blame. We have unnecessarily prolonged the existence of a land use control device conceived in another era when the true and frightening complexity of urban life was barely appreciated."[15] Unfortunately for me, the American Planning Association and La Blanca Gente's Town Clerk still believe that zoning is gospel, that zoning is what planners "do." For my part, at least, it appears I have an opportunity to prove Ava wrong.

4

Planning Incompetence

---

week after arriving in La Blanca Gente, I find myself sitting with my wife on an early June, mountain valley Sunday evening—the eve of my first day as the Town of La Blanca Gente's Community Development Director. All the boxes are unpacked, our modest belongings, a hodge-podge of furniture as accumulated over an eight-year relationship, are all neatly organized where one might expect.

We rent our manufactured home for $750 a month. In more informal lingo, it's known as a "double-wide." We would perhaps feel a bit more self conscious about living in what amounts to a trailer but, seeing as half the Town of La Blanca Gente shares our very same predicament, we found it to be socially acceptable.

The real estate market in La Blanca Gente had entered into the speculation phase of the maturation process previous to our arrival. Speculation always precedes growth but does not necessarily guarantee it. Just less than one-half of the town is undeveloped vacant parcels, all of which are covered in sagebrush and perhaps even a pine-tree or two. Many land-owners find it more cost effective to purchase a manufactured home and haul it into town to rest upon the parcel(s) they have purchased. Because land is so expensive there are many instances where the value of the land exceeds the value of the manufactured home.

My wife and I sit on our back deck and share a bottle of cabernet and a smoke or two. We gaze past our brown, fenced-in yard to Coyote Peak—the tallest, closest mountain to town at 11,500 feet, the peak of which is just a hair below Colorado alpine. Although it is about 80 degrees where Caitlin and I sit, Coyote Peak is still snow-capped—fruits of a moist La Blanca Gente winter.

The cabernet we sip calms my anxiety. The first day of the rest of my life starts in a mere matter of hours, and I know little of what to expect. It is evenings like this that shape a person. Years of irresponsibility, which preceded years of higher education, which preceded my sitting out on this deck, sipping a bottle of booze with my beloved wife, gazing at the snow-capped San Juan Mountains, a subsidiary of the Rocky Mountains, feeling as though, had fate twisted differently, I could just have easily been sitting in a jail cell at this very moment. Appropriately, on the eve of me officially becoming an adult, I'm going to get drunk in the meantime.

Caitlin and I chat about the reality before us as our wine glasses lighten. The setting sun signals that it was time to retreat to the comforts of our living room. Daughter fast asleep, we watched the *Sopranos* and talked little the rest of the evening before we drifted off to sleep.

Daylight shot through our bedroom windows around 5:15 in the morning. Summer mornings in La Blanca Gente are a sight to behold. The thin air's sun quickly scourers the Banshee of night. The mountain air is full of life as all those living recognize that La Blanca Gente summers are always fleeting, and time is of the essence.

I rise out of bed about 7:00 AM, too anxious to take advantage of a few extra minutes sleep. Not needing to be at work until 8:30, I shower and then sit on the couch like a lout and watch the *Today Show* to kill some time. Pondering the dismal state of American journalism, Caitlin rouses me in an effort to document the moment. Taking a few pictures of me dressed like a professional in slacks and button-up shirt, indeed moments like these, just minutes from starting my first adult job, can either be compared to a birth or a funeral; the effects are equally profound either way.

As 8:20 AM rolled around I decided it was time to stuff one pant sleeve into my sock, hop on my mountain bike—the Cinder Cone—and pedal the four blocks to Town Hall. Upon my arrival at 8:22 AM, I discovered Town Hall to be absent a bike rack (perhaps due to the lack of demand?), so I locked my front tire to the frame of my bike and rested both against the side of the building.

Ava's blue Subaru Forester was already parked outside, signaling her presence. Greeted by Bistro, a stray dog Ava adopted, upon entering Town Hall, I quickly made the five strides through the "lobby" to Ava's office.

We sat in her office, drank a cup of bitter and bodiless coffee, and small-talked for perhaps half an hour. When the conversation ran its course, Ava's six-foot tall frame stood and showed me around La Blanca Gente's Town Hall.

Three offices, a reception area, kitchen, and bathroom later, we arrived back in Ava's office. "So what do I do now?" I asked.

"I have some paperwork—retirement, health, town personnel policy, and the like—for you to look through and sign. You might want to browse around your office and perhaps tidy-up." Ava's suggestion triggered a remark to myself that went something like, "Why the hell isn't my office clean already?"

"Sounds good." I said as I grabbed a pile of paperwork and brought it back to my desk.

And so it went, the first day of the rest of my life was spent cleaning an office, deciphering insurance policies, and reading what appeared to be a surprisingly restrictive personnel policy. Luckily, as I left Town Hall, I happily noticed one of only two liquor stores in town was located across the street from my place of employment. Carrying a six pack of IPA in one hand, and steering the Cinder Cone with the other, I pondered an uneventful first day and was a bit curious as to why the town's Marketing Director, the Chief of Police, and at least one or two town elected officials did not take a moment to stop by and welcome me to the job.

Resting on the familiar argument, "there just isn't enough money to pay a skilled city manager," the town has gone without and in the meantime eagerly underpaid the rest of their personnel. The good news, however, is that in the absence of a city manager, all other "department heads" share equal power. I believe such a theory was explored in the Articles of Confederation but the less said about that the better.

I arrived to work the following morning and surfed the Internet for about an hour. Ava poked her head into my office to ask how things were going. We exchanged some chit-chat for awhile when the conversation finally turned to planning La Blanca Gente. "Just from first glance," I said, trying my best to sound like an expert, "the fundamental source of La Blanca Gente dysfunctionality stems from a lack of pedestrian orientation. The town has no center, no 'Main Street' for one to stroll and take in the environment."

Ava responded with her own version of an expert opinion, stating: "That coupled with a town full of dip shits, and you just hit the nail on the head."

"Is there a zoning code I can look through?" I asked less because I was interested and more because I was bored.

"Yes, there's the town's land use code, but we just hired a consultant out of Denver to write a new land use code, so I wouldn't bother learning too much from this one." Ava's information was quite priceless considering that I'm the Community Development Director or, as Ava sees it, the "Land Use Administrator."

"Is there a draft of the new code floating around?"

"Ya, I'll get you a copy."

"Sounds good," I said, now feeling a sense of real responsibility. My morale rose at the prospect of critiquing La Blanca Gente's draft land use code.

I didn't even acknowledge Ava as she placed a copy on my desk, too preoccupied to notice. The fluids in my brain started to circulate at an increased rate as the real significance of the moment hit me: no better place to create a pedestrian friendly town than the town's zoning code.

The Town of La Blanca Gente recently received a grant from the Colorado Department of Local Affairs in an effort to hire a consultant to write an entirely new code. With only $20,000 in their pocket, the La Blanca Gente Town Board pulled in Le Corbusier and Associates to run the show. Twenty-thousand dollars is not much money to underwrite such an endeavor. A town could easily spend two-hundred grand to do the task right. Likely out of pity, and perhaps a testament to La Blanca Gente's past incompetence, the Colorado Department of Local Affairs was kind enough to throw $20,000 our way for a new code.

Le Corbusier and Associates is a national planning firm. It takes a lot of contracts to finance such an operation and, without a doubt, addressing La Blanca Gente's zoning needs is not the sexiest of projects.

I was hopeful as I picked up the draft code. I massaged the cover page, knowing full well it was my new baby. At only 110 pages, the code would not take long to read in between distractions. Visions of sidewalks and bike-lanes flashed through my head. Zeroed out set-backs, tree lined streets, an architectural theme, anything and everything to make the pedestrian feel more at home. To invite the passer-by to step out for a stroll, perhaps even open his wallet at a business or two. The possibilities were endless.

La Blanca Gente straddles two state highways intersecting in the heart of town. Highway 2—Heaven's Highway—T's into Highway 1. La Blanca Gente's legal boundaries hug both highways, creating a three-pronged municipal geography that looks much like a boomerang. Heaven's Highway and Highway 1 are La Blanca Gente. Both are two-lane roads without sidewalks. There are buildings along both highways but they are not connected by any rhyme or reason. None of them relate to one another functionally or esthetically, unless you count the lack of rhyme or reason as their connection. Subdivisions squirrel off both highways into mazes of cul-de-sacs and dead ends. Not one subdivision within town is connected to another via a road that is not one of the highways. Heaven's Highway and Highway 1 are La Blanca Gente, and I intended to make both better.

Trouble is the Colorado Department of Transportation (CDOT) has jurisdiction over land use policy as it relates to their state highways. CDOT's primary goal is vehicle flow. Their mission statement expresses such a notion without regard to the toll it takes on towns like La Blanca Gente: "To provide the best multi-modal transportation system for Colorado that most effectively moves people, goods, and information."[16] Because, in La Blanca Gente, or if you're any other small town in Colorado with a state highway or two dissecting your city limits, it is not the home municipality that dictates what one can or can't do with your highway, it's engineers from CDOT. Like a pimp to a prostitute, CDOT owns our ass.

If there was an award for the narrowest minded, most one-dimensional thinkers, transportation engineers would win it. They don't think beyond, as Allan Jacobs says, ". . . the functional purposes of permitting people to get from one place to another and to gain access to property, streets—most assuredly the best streets—can and should help do other things."[17]

In the simple minds of CDOT Transportation Engineers, streets are for cars and, Goddamnit, they're going to move them as quickly and efficiently as possible, even if it takes twenty lanes and no sidewalks to do it.

Jacobs outlines eight characteristics, all of which can be isolated and observed but must be used in aggregate, which are incorporated into his classification of "Great Streets." Places for people to walk with some leisure, physical comfort, definition, qualities that engage the eyes, transparency, complementarity, maintenance, and quality of construction and design— all must sing in harmony to create an Allan Jacobs' Great Street, and I don't disagree with him.[18] Such qualities are all absent along La Blanca Gente's two most visible and traveled streets. What can be seen from La Blanca Gente's two highways defines the image of La Blanca Gente. Sadly, such an image may not be influenced by me or the La Blanca Gente Town Board. No, it's defined by CDOT engineers that care little about creating community and care more about allowing traffic to flow as quickly and efficiently as possible. Jacobs would not be pleased.

I spent the next two days reading and re-reading the draft code. As I drew every word into my mind, and my thoughts began to crystallize around them, the irony of the situation became more and more clear: this is a document that will hurt La Blanca Gente more than it will help it.

Classic nonsense, the code is a microcosm of everything that's wrong with planning. Developing to its standards would mean each development, from a single family home to a hundred unit subdivision, would stand without consideration to their relationships with their surrounding landscape—built or physical. Each development would be considered in isolation unto itself, with total subordination to vehicular access without even a passing tip-of-the-hat to the pedestrian or bicyclist.

Andres Duany, et al. said it best in *Suburban Nation*: "Even the classic American main street, with its mixed-use buildings right up against the sidewalk, is now illegal in most municipalities. Somewhere along the way, through a series of well-intentioned steps, traditional towns became a crime in America."[19] Such is the case in La Blanca Gente should this code become law.

I get the sense that the folks from Le Corbusier and Associates simply plucked an already written land use code from one of their hard-drives and submitted it to Ava and the Town of La Blanca Gente. We had been conned out of $20,000 and received nothing more than fool's gold. The Department of Commerce' Standard Enabling Act, a relic from 1924, is stamped all over this thing. Without even a hint of New Urbanism, this document will shape La Blanca Gente in the vision of a suburban utopia perched at 8,200 feet without even a mother city to suckle from.

It all starts with the usual language: General Provisions, Administration, and then advances quickly into Subdivision and Zoning

Regulations.[20] Andres Duany and the gang would not be pleased.

"Ava!" I hollered from my desk to her office, which is not more than ten paces away.

"What is it?"

"Who wrote this drivel? I'm embarrassed to read such nonsense. In fact, I think I'm stupider because of it."

"Le Corbusier and Associates wrote the document. They're supposed to be experts." Ava said as she appeared in my office.

"Who's the lead consultant working with us?" I asked.

"Kirby Shroyt. He's up in Denver." Ava responded. "What's wrong with the code?"

"This thing's a recipe for disaster. It has absolutely no consideration for the pedestrian and what such considerations entail from an urban design perspective."

"That's not such a big deal," Ava said while pretending to wipe the dust off the top of my computer monitor, "no one walks in this town, anyway."

I responded quickly, and with a smirk on my face said, "No one walks in this town because this town was not built for walkers. This code does nothing to address that."

"Ya, that may be the case, but Kirby's the expert. I think we should stick with what he suggests." Ava responded to me as she walked out of my office to answer the phone.

"It's a shit code, Ava," was the only response I could muster.

Kirby's the expert, huh? Judging by the merits of this code, Kirby, evidently, does not give a shit about La Blanca Gente. Any planner worth his salt can easily see, without any mental strain or creativity, the planning oriented challenges that strewn across La Blanca Gente's landscape like cards on a poker table. If Hungry Mind ever published an *Urban Planning for Dummies*, La Blanca Gente would be the most-cited example of how not to do things. This code represents the antitheses of planning. Is Kirby so used up and dried out that he's lost all drive to try and change things? Or, does he just not know any better? Regardless of the unanswered questions, the only expert that has touched this code, despite Ava's opinion, is me.

Ava gave me Kirby's number, and I called directly. I left him a voicemail, and tried to sound chipper in doing so. Yet to achieve satisfaction, I thought it best to hone my anger into a memo that totally and thoroughly cut into Kirby's draft code with the precision of an assassin.

I doubt not that you know the concepts of New Urbanism/smart growth as well as I, but for the sake of argument, let's run through them together: mixed land uses, moderate to high density development, mixed incomes, zeroed-out set-backs, pedestrian-friendly first and vehicle-friendly second; I just can't understand why some people find these concepts so complex, particularly Kirby Shroyt? In La Blanca Gente's draft code, the land uses, generally classified as commercial, residential, and industrial, are strictly separated. Downtowns and neighborhood centers once thrived because residential units were built atop commercial units. When post World War II zoning spread like a cancer, in conjunction with the rise of the automobile, central cities inadvertently paved the way for the middle class to flee the city for shiny new single family subdivisions, built on the fringe (and mostly outside the taxable city limits) of town. Everyone who could afford it left for what appeared to be greener pastures, leaving in their wake the stench of poverty. Now a significant distance from their day-to-day needs, these new homeowners found they had to drive to work, drive to get a loaf of bread, drive to achieve whatever their hearts desired.

Methodically, these growing suburbs incorporated into "cities" or were annexed by adjacent towns; the government corporations imposed zoning codes that protected the "culture of the community." The rise of the enclosed shopping mall tried to fulfill suburbanites' need for all the amenities that a "Main Street" once provided. Office complexes sprouted along major suburban corridors, only furthering the decline of central business districts because now suburbanites had absolutely no reason to travel downtown.

Urban Revitalization 101's primary philosophy is to bring the residential uses back to once thriving commercial centers. When the people come back, so too does the commercial space. Some might argue, although chances are they don't know why, that land uses should be strictly segregated. The roots of such narrow thinking stem back to Euclidian zoning, and the merits of segregating the smelters and hog farms from everything else. Indeed, most industrial uses should be segregated as a matter of public health, but does it really matter if someone wants to live astride office or retail space?

Density is key, too. In the suburbs, one must drive to obtain goods and services. In a high density, mixed-use environment, there's always a good and a service right around the corner, which is a nice segue into my Jane Jacobs citation. In *The Death and Life of Great American Cities*, Jacobs explains the virtue of density by stating, "In a given geographical territory, half as many people will not support half as many such enterprises spaced at twice the distance. When distance inconvenience sets in, the small, the various, and the personal whither away."[21] You know as well as I do the charisma of the suburbs pales in comparison to neighborhoods that were built before the automobile and zoning standards took the "sexy" out of "city."

Encouraging mixed incomes reduces crime. High concentrations of low income families are where the bad neighborhoods are, not because the families are poor, but because there's high crime. This is perhaps the most challenging concept for municipalities to adopt. Extremely progressive cities such as Portland, Oregon, and Montgomery, Maryland, have provisions in their land use codes that either stimulate or require developers to include low-income housing in all new residential developments.[22] Shit, the Communist Republic of California has low income housing requirements written into their state statues.[23] Naturally, under the guise of political correctness, the proper term to use when referring to residential units that serve the low-income marketplace is "affordable housing."

Zeroing-out set backs, particularly front and side set backs, insures buildings will be built to the sidewalk to engage the pedestrian. The first reaction to such a notion is, "where will people park?" Because your typical 20-foot commercial set back happens to be the average length of a parking stall, developers intuitively started using such space to fulfill parking requirements, and thus the strip mall was born. With little to no disagreement from planners, your best bet is to bring those buildings back to the sidewalk and allow developers to place their parking behind their buildings or, even better, allow for creative parking remedies, such as those suggested by Donald C. Shoup in his book *The High Cost of Free Parking*, and then your city will hum with activity once again.

There are a million other factors to consider when attempting to put together a strident land use code that actually stimulates the function of a city rather than Kirby Shroyt's draft code, which would ultimately retard the function of La Blanca Gente. Geographer Gundars Rudzitis says it best, though, in *Wilderness and the Changing American West*: "To maintain the uniqueness of an area such as the wilderness West, in a dynamic sense, is to increase its viability by development that maintains or improves the quality of life by fitting harmoniously into the natural and cultural environment."[24]

New Urbanism, smart growth, or whatever you want to call it, has evolved to such a degree over the past 15 years it is now a rather exact science, perhaps too exact. Real estate developers have largely recognized the virtues (profit potential) of New Urbanism in their own twisted, capitalistic way. Calling such enclaves "life-style centers" or "outdoor malls," such places follow a strict recipe of tenant mix and use type, mostly courtesy of the International Council of Shopping Centers—the industry's key professional organization. God bless their hearts for at least getting it half right, but such places are so over planned, it creates a utopic, Disney-like atmosphere. Such new developments, which now pepper the country, may contain many of the key tenants of New Urbanism, but what they fail to do is create an atmosphere of the unexpected, of diversity. There is no magic. Where's the bum on the corner trying to pan-handle some change? Where's the dirty old hippie strumming a guitar on the sidewalk? Where's the random group of thugs that you're trying your best not to make eye-contact with? Where's the guy in the $2,000 dollar suit walking alongside a janitor who's on his lunch break, too?

To extend a term Richard Florida uses in *The Rise of the Creative Class,* "generica" best describes many of these New Urbanist enclaves that exercise a strict mix of commercial (mostly national) retail tenants and perhaps, if a developer is forward thinking enough, a handful of residential uses. Florida applies the term to the commercialization of experiences aimed at attracting the creative class market. How does a developer, retailer, club, restaurant, and you name it create a perfectly organic and indigenous experience every day or night of the week? More daunting yet, how does one plan for the indigenous and the organic? Commercialization does indeed create place generica. All a planner can do is put the proper mix of ingredients together, such as different establishments that drive different activity in different parts of the day and serve different market segments or, as the industry likes to call it, different "psychographics."

We need the bohemians mixing with the WASP's, business people mixing with the hippies. Punks, gang bangers, goths, baby boomers, thugs, bums, artists, the elite, old money, new money, homosexuals, heterosexuals, fat people, skinny people, gym rats, and drug addicts; different attractions attract different people, and all a planner can do is try to put in place an appropriate balance of attractions. Some attractions may be national chains, other attractions may be low-rent studio space. Without belaboring the point any further, if developers are in charge of determining the tenant mix on large scale projects, generica will come of it.

I almost hesitate to say it because I don't know if I believe it, but, at least for the large scale (re)development projects, instead of controlling the land-uses, perhaps the public sector should control the tenant mix? The implications of which are a bit too complex to explore at this time. The point is, however, the perfectly planned, perfectly functional urban place would look a lot like the streets of Calcutta, only with better landscaping: a mess of people from every class and background utilizing the city's space. Although many of the developer-driven New Urban enclaves deserve credit for getting planning half-right, such places are little more than a destination for the upper-middle class to shop, and for singles with plenty of disposable income to reside. "Real" does not happen until an element of "unpredictable" becomes reality. How does a planner plan for the unpredictable? Furthermore, if it's planned for, one could argue that "unpredictable" is no longer a relevant term to describe the concept.

Kirby Shroyt had an opportunity to fix La Blanca Gente, to save the town from its own deep malaise of planning ignorance. He could have submitted a draft land use code that totally re-thought the status quo of town development, and he could have gotten away with it, too, because he's the outside expert. He has all the credibility. Whatever he would have submitted as a first draft would have been considered typical. He could have submitted a 110 page New Urbanist code, and no one would have known any better, they would have accepted the draft as gospel, tinkered around with some words, and, in the end, adopted a kick-ass pedestrian friendly code. Fate is not so kind to Tedesco, however. Fortuna's Wheel spun me downward the day Kirby Shroyt decided to make $20,000 the easy way.

Now, I'm pitted against the expert. I'm the instigator, the radical, all because someone who should have known better submitted a document more fit for suburban Los Angeles than scenic La Blanca Gente.

If you're a planner, or even if you're one who has a passing fascination with cities and how they work, New Urbanism and smart growth are no longer mysterious. You don't need a Shaman to implement them, all you need is a city council with sack enough to adopt such policies and a planning department with the savvy to make them think it's a good idea.

5

Relationship Building

As early summer drifted into mid-summer, with snow on the peaks thinning by the day, the relationship between Ava and me deteriorated drastically. I avoided any and all conversations with her. Like a politician, when I did have to speak with her, I chose my words carefully.

Keeping to myself, I kept busy by writing a grant for a proposed museum and dealing with whatever else popped up, which wasn't much. My professional attitude sunk into a state of confusion and unhappiness. It wasn't supposed to be this way. It was supposed to be fun. It was supposed be much simpler. Sadly, however, I find Ava to be a road block between me and the Town Board for every great idea that I brought to the table.

I now know Ava well enough to know that I am terrified of what she is capable of doing to me. My open-mindedness toward her in the beginning of our professional relationship has been chiseled away through her constantly correcting me, and generally hovering around me waiting for a mistake. Now she's just an irritant, an obstacle to be strategically dealt with through back-room discussions and, as much as possible, simply ignoring her.

The deterioration of our relationship started innocently enough. The Town Hall conference room, for instance, where the Town Board conducts their work sessions, is filled with a conference room table and enough space for perhaps 12 chairs for those who have the motivation to attend public meetings. Like clock work, at the work sessions, I would invite myself to sit at the conference room table alongside Ava and the rest of the Town Board. My theory being that if the Town Clerk has a seat at the big boys' table, than why not the Community Development Director? Unfortunately, my theoretical construct insulted Ava by affronting her sense of control. Because, as the Town Board would ask general administrative questions, I would chime up before Ava had the opportunity. It wasn't three meetings before Ava confronted me one day and said, "Mike, during work sessions, the conference room table is reserved for the Town Board and me, so I can take the minutes." From then on, I sat in the gallery with the rest of the peasants.

Or perhaps it's the fact that I'm a social butterfly. The La Blanca Gente business community latched onto me like a spoon to a magnet. Indeed, grateful that there was an alternative attitude in Town Hall rather than Ava's, who had been acting as the interim Community Development Director in addition to her duties as Town Clerk, they welcomed me as an alcoholic welcomes a bottle. In conjunction with my popularity with the La Blanca Gente civic elite, people no longer walked into Town Hall looking for Ava. No, they walked in looking for me.

Possibly it was the fact that I snubbed Ava's "Town Hall community coffee" and brought in my own gourmet coffee, as well as a French Press to help make it. Such an effort may have been construed as snobbery. Then again, who knows?

Maybe it was my attempt to totally redefine what La Blanca Gente planners "do" that stimulated the negative aspects of my relationship with Ava. Before me, she only dealt with opinionless "Land Use Administrators" whose only responsibility was to administrate the town's land use code. My predecessors were easily manipulated by Ava and, therefore, controlled. On the other hand, I am an entirely new entity, a "Community Development Director" who has actually read a book or two on urban planning, not to mention the many ambiguous facets of my being. To me, my land use responsibilities were secondary to my economic development responsibilities. To Ava, however, I had no economic development responsibilities.

Or perhaps it was the fact that Ava had always run Town Hall her way. Now, she has to put up with some strange kid who has a different perception on how to conduct business, who tends to have an optimistic attitude, and has an ego large enough to swallow a battleship.

Somehow, Ava put me on her no-fly list, and I doubted whether or not I could get off. Maybe, actually, most probably, it was the fact that I represented change. Change in the way La Blanca Gente's Planning Department conducted business, change in the way La Blanca Gente town administrators conducted business, change in the way Town Hall's new perception of La Blanca Gente is that of potential, if it could only be harnessed for good, rather than create problems. The difference between me and most La Blanca Gente locals is the locals have an uncanny ability to gripe about all the perceived problems with their town. I am more than happy to sit right along with them to state my opinions regarding the challenges that face La Blanca Gente. The difference, though, is I would actually spend time trying to fix the problems everybody gripes about, not just content myself to simple complaints with no action behind them.

The entire culture of La Blanca Gente is quite astonishing, really. An anthropologist could conduct an enthnograph on La Blanca Gente and it would be as significant as when that one white guy ethnographed a purely "untouched" Amazon tribe in the 1960s. Except, now, I'm the one trying to dance around the fire and it looks totally out of place. I'm glad the camera crew stayed home.

It must be instinctual, some highly evolved (or highly recessed) gene that is only dominant in La Blanca Gente. Everyone complains, but no one stands up and says, "how do we fix it?" Full of problems but short on solutions. Even the La Blanca Gente Board of Trustees, the seven La

Blanca Gente residents in the best position to fix problems, was reluctant to even publicly confront and identify said problems. Because, by doing so, the local gossip circle—including Ava—would start to identify them as the problem. It's like picking on your sister—it's okay if you do it, but if someone else does it then it's grounds for an ass-kicking.

In La Blanca Gente, feel free to throw your logic out the window. Logic and rational thinking are moot, if not criticized. Taken as a whole, the residents of La Blanca Gente are a faithless people. Even using the term "logic" is grounds for a crucifixion. To Ava and, indeed, her circle of influence, I have become part of the problem. Something new to bemoan because everything else has been bemoaned to death. A man with a target on my back, a little red dot on my forehead. The hyenas have separated me from the pack.

Indeed, the harbinger that summer was already half spent, was the annual Cowboy Days festival slated to start over the weekend. Required to work the event, and managed by La Blanca Gente's Marketing Director, I served sodas for a buck a piece out of a vending booth all weekend long. On Sunday afternoon, only hours away from the conclusion of the event, a classic Southwest monsoon thunderstorm came upon the town like the eighth plague of Egypt. Lightning flashed all around. In my metal cocoon, I felt a bit insecure. There were others, however, without the luxury of shelter. Like a swarm of ants just roused by a child's stick, people scattered in all directions as the rain and lightning crashed around us.

At the height of the storm, a bolt of lightning struck only yards away from Town Hall, which is only a block from where Cowboy Days was taking place. The storm served as an appropriate metaphorical crescendo for Cowboy Days as well as the opening salvo in the "I Hate You but We're Not Going to Talk about It" period with Ava.

When I walked into the office on Monday, Ava was about to have a heart attack. Franticly darting from computer to computer, she told me that none of the computers were working. I walked into my office and turned mine on. Soon after I could smell the fragrance of burning wires and electrical equipment. My computer was blown. I turned it off and did what I could to help Ava with her state of fanaticism. Intentionally, but giving the illusion it was unintentional, I made the effort to get in her way and just generally add to her Monday morning frustration. I was, honestly, quite happy my computer got hit because it was old and slow and that is cause enough to drive a person into therapy. That morning I dreamt of the kick-ass new computer I knew I would be getting.

In the meantime, the town's Marketing Director—Tami Inanis— helped Ava jimmy-rig a make-shift computer to place in Ava's office. For Tami's part, she brought in her personal lap-top. Both Tami and Ava had access to the Internet. The Chief of Police, for whatever reason, preferred a type writer to a computer, so he didn't much miss the technology. Of all the department heads, I was the odd man out, left without a computer to work on or an Internet to surf on. I was in a lurch. My guess was that this thrilled Ava.

It would be two and a half months before I finally received a computer for my office. It was the slowest, most agonizing period of my young life. No Internet at home, and no Internet in my office, my umbilical cord to the rest of the world was temporarily cut. I did not have Internet at home because I refused to pay $40 a month for freakin' dial-up, which at the time was the only Internet service in the La Blanca Gente market. Town Hall Internet access bounces off a satellite tower, and we paid a premium for it. Not only did I not have office Internet access, I did not even have a computer. At first, facing such a disparaging reality—eight hours a day with no computer moping around Town Hall—appeared to be a prison sentence. Until, right around 3:00 PM the second day, literally sitting in my office twiddling my thumbs, I got up and told Ava, "I'm going to go home and use my computer to get some work done."

"You can't do that unless you get authorization," she replied, as she looked up at me from her computer screen.

"Authorization from whom?"

"The Town Board," was her response.

"Do you really expect me to wait for the next board meeting to ask permission to be more productive?"

"That's not the issue, Mike. The issue is you would like to work from home."

"Need I remind you why it is that I would like to work from home?"

"No, but I suspect that a more creative person would be able to find a way to be productive without a computer at work," Ava said.

"You don't have a whole lot of credibility arguing that point, Ava, considering that you have a working computer on your desk. Furthermore, creativity has nothing to do it; productivity is the issue, so I am going to make an administrative decision to utilize my time a bit more productively."

We stared at each other for a moment both awaiting the next volley. I left, went home, and ended up dozing-off in front of my computer.

Such was my routine for the next couple of months: come to work at 8:30, dink around with a cup of coffee in my hands for the next several hours and, by lunch, I was at home happily plugging away on my computer and eventually taking a nice afternoon nap. Aside from the lack of external access to the universe, not a bad interim gig, really. I sensed that it really pissed Ava off, too.

I'm no expert, just a guy with too many bad habits, but half the trouble with planning and, indeed, generally being employed by a local government, is you may be an expert, and you may have some knowledge, but knowledge and expertise is moot much of the time because the populace elected seven people that are not you to make decisions for the town, and those seven people only have you around to implement their own stupidity.

To purchase five new computers for the Town of La Blanca Gente, something that should have taken a week, took two and a half months. In the meantime, I'm at home taking naps, and not really getting anything done while I'm in the office, anyway, but the people elected to be the responsible stewards of La Blanca Gente municipal tax dollars approached the computer situation like they were plotting the invasion of Mexico.

Town staff and a couple of interested Town Board members worked with a tech consultant to create a list of the town's computer needs. I was insulted they even hired a tech consultant. They could have just had a conversation with me and saved themselves the $2,000. Within the computer list, I was the only one who requested a lap-top. I knew this would cause trouble.

"This isn't Christmas, Mike. You'll get what you'll get," Ava barked.

"Thanks for the calendar update, Ava. Your opinions aside, I'll just as soon take my chances requesting a lap-top."

We set a work session to hammer out the budget for the new computers and give the bosses a chance to express their opinions. Over my time in La Blanca Gente, I've realized that the work sessions are where all the real decisions are made. The official Town of La Blanca Gente Board of Trustees' meetings are just an act to go through the required statutory motions to make decisions official.

I knew that at the up-coming work session I might get hammered for requesting a lap-top. Worse yet, I knew the odds were against me because the Town Board is not necessarily filled with tech-savvy individuals—some don't even have email accounts. Also, and more importantly, I knew Ava was working behind the scenes to kill my request. If I had half a brain, I would have been working the backrooms, too. A couple of strategic phone calls would have served me well.

During the meeting, Ava did her part to try to subvert my request. "He's requesting a portable," she said. "What if it gets stolen? Every address in town would be on that computer."

I lofted a volley in response: "I'm told it's critically important for identity thieves to know the zoning for a person's property in order to attain their social security number." A chuckle or two eased the atmosphere. "Communities across the country utilize lap-tops to help make their employees more productive. If the only argument against the lap-top is a fear of thieves obtaining the zoning information, which is public information to begin with, for every property in town, then I would say the seven of you have nothing to worry about."

Astonishingly, they bought my argument. Nodding their heads in unison, the Town Board agreed to buy it for me. In the next couple of days Ava collected bids from three different computer companies, although, at the work session, the Town Board had already decided what outfit to order computers from. Once Ava met all of the procurement requirements to make a large purchase, such as a slue of new computers, she received the green light from the Town Board to order them.

Days past. I did not want to ask Ava if she had ordered the computers. I felt more comfortable assuming that she was as eager as I was to order them. I assumed that Ava, for her own sake at least, needed to get the office back to normal. Five days past. Waiting for a sign, I finally asked Ava if she had ordered them. She said, "No, Mike, I haven't gotten to it yet." The next day I asked her again: "Have you ordered the computers yet?"

"Nope, haven't gotten to it," Ava said as she was just beginning to sit down behind her make-shift computer. I left Town Hall that day considering my options.

That night, there was a regular meeting of the Town Board. Toward the end of every meeting, there is an "Operations Highlights" portion of the agenda set aside for all town department heads to explain what they have been doing for the past month. I took the opportunity to railroad Ava at a public meeting in front of all seven bosses and a few random members of the public. When it was my turn to speak, I efficiently and calmly explained what I had been doing for the past month. Then, I launched into a tirade: "It has been six days since Ava was given the green light to order new computers. She still has not ordered them. I'm letting all you know that I cannot function without a computer. I need a computer as soon as possible. Ava, when are you going to order the new computers?" The room was dead silent as it searched for an answer.

"I ordered them today, and thanks for asking."

"Well thank you, Ava, for being so generous with your time." The meeting ended. I felt pretty good because I was able to vent some frustrations to the Town Board, piss Ava off, embarrass her in public, and display the fact that she pushed me too far on the freakin' computers.

The next morning I showed up to the office and worked on whatever I needed to do, which wasn't much without a computer.

Choosing the term "spoiled brat" as her ammunition, not long later, Tami came strutting into my office with a chip on her shoulder and a fight to pick.

6

Marketing Incompetence

I've always been of the opinion that city planning is a field far-flung from architecture. It is mystifying to think that architects are more qualified to plan cities than, say, geographers, sociologists, or even civil engineers. Architecture is a peculiar field because it represents the marriage between empirical and subjective studies. If a building functions perfectly yet looks atrocious, has the architect failed or succeeded? Perhaps, because geographers, sociologists, and civil engineers do not get the luxury of subjective analysis per se, the architect can stake rightful claim as urban planner. If we look closer, however, it is revealed the architect resides over an illusionary fiefdom. The product of historical inertia and coincidence, architects took the budding field of urban planning and pasted it as a branch on their own academic tree.

In large part, urban planners can thank the City Beautiful Movement for allowing their field to migrate into the hands of the intellectual braggarts. The City Beautiful Movement, driven by business and bourgeois elitists pulling the strings, tended to disregard the working class and narrowly focused on the superficial notion of architecture—via Roman and Greek neoclassical—as the one-stop cure-all for the ills of urban living.

There are brief moments in history that will forever be cited as revolutionary. Columbus's accidental landing on a small Caribbean island, the first Continental Congress, man walking on the moon, and, as it pertains to the subject at hand, the World's Columbian Exposition of 1893. It was there, on the streets of Chicago overlooking Lake Michigan, that the world was re-introduced to classical Greek and Roman architecture. The White City, it was dubbed, and its mayor was Daniel Burnham. The patron saint of the City Beautiful Movement, Burnham designed cities and buildings from San Francisco to New York. His magna carta, however, was implemented in the same city that brought him fame: Chicago. It was here that the City Beautiful Movement came into fruition with Burnham's Chicago Plan of 1909.

The Chicago Plan represents the goals of City Beautiful. The plan was to rigidify ". . . the chaotic city that had arisen through too-rapid growth and too-rich mixture of nationalities, would be given order by cutting new thoroughfares, removing slums, and extending parks."[25] The City Beautiful Movement's main objectives are seen as ". . . a concerted effort to bring focus and unity where chaos, visual squalor, or monotony has reigned."[26] To achieve these goals, the prescription called for a very architectural theme of aesthetics.

The turn of the century was to be "ushered in with a blaze of neoclassical glory"[27] unheard of since Europe crawled out of the Middle Ages. The City Beautiful Movement would cure the ills of urban life simply by making cities look better. The logic of the movement clearly stems from architectural principles—make buildings look beautiful. It would be difficult to argue that the structures that were conceived and built in the era were not spectacular pieces of work that do deserve much praise. But, predicate the design plan of a city on aesthetics alone? That is akin to blasphemy and it comes as no surprise that the infidels who pushed this prescription were architects. Perhaps this is why Jane Jacobs called the City Beautiful Movement an "architectural design cult."[28]

The goals of City Beautiful were not misplaced; they were mis-prioritized. It is easy to see why the movement garnered support. The simple directive of making buildings look nice, predicated on the tried and true model of classical architecture, was a sure thing. The poor and working classes were brushed aside in the name of civic pride while the middle class elite reaped the benefits. As seen in Burnham's 1909 Chicago plan, the business community backed City Beautiful because, illustrated by Haussmann's Paris, "City Beautiful proved a good investment."[29]

The narrow focus of City Beautiful works out well for architects; the problem is, however, cities are a dynamic far larger than pleasing geometries. The latter day saints of city planning, Andres Duany, Elizabeth Platter-Zyberk, and Jeff Speck, criticize City Beautiful in this respect. "The successes of turn of the century planning, represented in America by the City Beautiful Movement, became the foundation of a new profession, and ever since, planners have repeatedly attempted to relive that moment of glory . . ."[30] The City Beautiful Movement was the planners' "moment of glory" simply because the business class elite saw this form of planning as a sound investment, rather than a form of government bureaucracy. Today, planners are more likely to be scorned as communists. The narrow focus of City Beautiful—to yield a prosperous business climate—is in stark contrast to what contemporary planners face in day-to-day practice.

Ironically, the City Beautiful Movement's greatest downfall is at the same time its only endowment. In today's urban environment, critics abound. Developers are notorious for placing profit above community design and, therefore, well-being. Retail powerhouses like Walmart feed off of the current suburban development status quo. Strip development fosters a culture of drive-by architecture with little community aesthetic characteristics other than its cookie-cutter commonality looks like every other place. As a result, many middle class urbanites suffer from what Douglas Coupland calls "terminal wanderlust—unable to feel rooted in any one environment, they [the middle class] move continually in the hopes of finding an idealized sense of community in the next location."[31] City Beautiful's narrow focus accomplished some of the most lasting architectural monuments America may ever see, and, consequently, they should be preserved for future generations.

It should be noted that at the exposition when the White City was introduced, Fredrick Jackson Turner declared the Western frontier closed. So, at the same time Turner closed one era, Burnham introduced a new more civil one. The remnants of which sit alongside gourmet coffee shops and microbreweries from Chicago to Seattle; as a result, Burnham's legacy was a vital part of the West's maturation process.

The City Beautiful Movement created memorable architecture and city-scapes. It is clear, though, that it was the product of architects, not planners. The consequences are hardly surprising. Is it any wonder that Burnham (the architect) is the patron saint of an urban design movement based solely on architecture? As planners, we should not be disappointed with the City Beautiful Movement; rather, we need to recognize it as a large scale manifestation of architecture. Simply, the City Beautiful Movement is an example of why architects should stick to architecture and let planners—people who are trained to stimulate the function of cities—deal with the design of cities.

Unfortunately, as planners, all the above points are largely academic when it comes to day to day municipal planning. Caught up in the hum-drum of "current planning" renders most planning theory impotent. So it goes in La Blanca Gente; depending on the week, upwards of 70% of my time was spent playing the bureaucrat rather than planning for more meaningful development.

As such, I'm forced to spend early mornings and nights attending meetings (unpaid, mind you) doing things most planners receive a six figure salary to do. But don't get me wrong; as much as it irritates me that my bosses don't know and, more importantly, don't compensate me for the job I do, after a couple years of doing hard time in La Blanca Gente, I'll be prepared to kick some serious planning ass in my next gig.

For now, however, La Blanca Gente is a low lying fruit. If it is to develop properly, it will need a taste of "La Blanca Gente Beautiful," and it all starts along the highway corridors. Obtaining the goal of smart development that compliments La Blanca Gente requires parting the sea of ignorance that stands between the town and where the town leaders say they want to go. The Town Clerk does not like me; the town Marketing Director does not like me; by virtue of their unwillingness to allow me to operate independent of their opinions, I've been forced to align myself with the pro-development cohort of the San Luis Valley—developers, real estate agents, pro-growth civic groups, etc. To a certain degree, I feel like I've sold my soul to the devil. In more traditional settings, developers are the ones whom are not to be trusted. Such is not the case in bizzaro La Blanca Gente. Politically, snuggling up to the money-hungry cohorts of the Valley is the right maneuver for two reasons: first, my bosses, although they constantly get in their own way, want development, and second, facilitating and manipulating the opinions of La Blanca Gente's moneyed elite should provide me with enough political cover to achieve smart development—my own little City Beautiful Movement.

Thus, as planners were to the City Beautiful Movement, it's me and my new-money posse positioning ourselves to create change. Ava, Tami, and their local gossip circle, no doubt, will influence the process. However, judging by their high level of ineptitude and senselessness, chances are they'll screw up before I do. Ava has an ally on the Town Board, however, that concerns me. Elroy Potus, Ava's lover, Ava's boss, Tami's boss, my boss. Ava tends to spend a couple hours each morning spreading the Gospel According to Ava about various topics, mostly town related, to Elroy. I've gotten used to her whispering and low, muffled tones while she talks with him. Considering I'm the only person within ear shot of her conversation, it's clear there is plenty she does not want me to hear. No matter, Elroy is only one vote of seven, which means Ava would have to sleep with three more bosses before they would have a majority willing to fire me.

The entire situation is perhaps unethical. Ava's in a position to subtly exercise undo power over, not only me, but all the town's employees via Elroy as her conduit. She and Elroy are "special friends," snuggling up on those cold La Blanca Gente nights under their own blanket of stupidity. Every time Elroy expresses an opinion at a public meeting, the question that must be asked of him is, "is this Elroy talking, or Ava?" To make matters worse, Elroy and Ava are two peas in a pod: both skeptics, both doing their part to hold the town back, both a couple of anti-Tedesco zealots. Over time, I came to learn that many of Ava's problems stem from a mindset that is paralyzed by the fear of being sued for whatever decisions are being made from Town Hall. Perhaps if she chose to pursue an education that afforded her a bit more credibility than a high school diploma, she would think differently. Alas, the Shelob has neither the ambition nor the confidence to sit through a few years of school, despite how well it might serve her. I came to learn that my only option, other than quitting and moving on, would be for her to get fired and therefore rid the town of her ineptitude and festering ignorance. Elroy is up for re-election come April; no doubt I will do my part to help ensure Elroy is no longer an obstacle to be considered.

What Ava, Elroy, and Tami don't know is that attracting development is not hard, particularly if there is a degree of population growth. La Blanca Gente has no primary industries; its economy rests uneasily on the one-legged stool of tourism. With Wolf Creek ski area just up the road and, not to mention, the vast assortment of high-country recreational opportunities, La Blanca Gente has a steady and predictable influence of tourist money.

Like that nerdy girl in middle school who blossomed into a beautiful woman in high school, La Blanca Gente finally got noticed by big-money real estate investors three years prior to my arrival. An 18-hole private golf club with additional spin-off residential units was the result. The Ty Webb Club, perched just outside of municipal La Blanca Gente, now attracts the seasonal home owner looking for "real Colorado" while they fight the nagging feeling in the back of their Texan heads that for each one of them that purchases property in or around La Blanca Gente, it becomes less and less real, and less and less Colorado.

The Texans come up during the summer to take a break from the heat. I've heard horror stories of how some Colorado mountain towns become so saturated with Texans during the summer months that Colorado State flags are replaced by the Lone Star, and they flap high above for everyone to see.

Not only did the Ty Webb Club change the trajectory of La Blanca Gente growth, there is the looming Village at Wolf Creek development on the horizon. The brain child of one Buckley Hasslbeck, the Village is an upper-class ski destination at the base of Wolf Creek ski area. Village, in this case, is a euphemism for small city, because the projected build-out of the Village at Wolf Creek is roughly 10,000 people.

Clearly, La Blanca Gente is on the cusp of tapping into the growth machine. So easy a kid could do it, it's only a matter of time before a wave of commercial growth floods the town. In order to create that wave, however, it's up to the leaders and residents of La Blanca Gente to walk into the water. Fully tapping into the recreational tourism industry by selling La Blanca Gente's natural amenities is only a step away. Taking that step, one deep breath before the plunge, is only a matter of choosing the right tool to do so.

The Town of La Blanca Gente operates on pennies. By no stretch of the imagination is the town coffer equipped to finance anything but the most basic of operations. Due to the absence of capital, the Town Board is left with little but their own creativity to stimulate development. Funding options at the state and Federal levels are numerous. Many of these options, however, are in the form of long term, low interest loans or grants that entail a matching contribution. The only way for these options to enter the realm of feasibility is if they are invested in a project that generates a hasty return.

Most La Blanca Gente residents are acutely aware that we need development. Where the arguments start, however, is deciding the appropriate scale and rate of such development; from the Village at Wolf Creek to a new shop opening in town, most residents rest their opinions somewhere along that scale. For La Blanca Gente, the pieces are in place, the board is nearly set; it's only a matter of time before the development game begins.

A critical piece of the development puzzle includes letting the world know that La Blanca Gente exists, and providing the information necessary for developers to start the consideration process of investing in La Blanca Gente. Toward that end, I worked in earnest researching and developing a commercial market analysis. Indeed, given the usual assortment of questions that go unanswered from developers, a commercial market analysis will prove helpful to disseminate information.

Tami, the town's Marketing Director, protected for the most part by the day-to-day office discomfort of Town Hall by virtue of her relative seclusion in the Visitors' Center, has a handful of facts and figures that may prove relevant.

I found myself walking into the office of a woman who, only a few days earlier, called me a spoiled brat for challenging Ava's management decisions.

"Hey Tami, you mentioned the other day in a meeting that Colorado is like the fourth or fifth most requested state for information regarding travel?" I asked, intentionally skipping the small talk. "I'm wondering if you have that exact figure and if you can get me the source on that so I can cite it?"

"What are you going to put it in?" Tami said to her computer screen.

"Well, as you know, I'm starting a real estate market analysis, and this is a good number to mention in there."

"Look," she said, finally looking up to acknowledge my presence. "As you know, I'm in charge of marketing La Blanca Gente. As such, I would appreciate it if you kept me in the loop on your market analysis considering that this is a task that falls within a fuzzy area between our job boundaries."

"How is a real estate market analysis considered marketing, Tami?"

"Because you intend to pass the document out in an effort to attract development."

"Are you concerned about how I distribute the report, Tami?"

"I'm concerned about why you're writing the report. You are aware that I'm the Marketing Director, right?"

"What is it, exactly, that the Town of La Blanca Gente's Marketing Director does?"

"One of the things I do, Mike, is market the town utilizing reports like the one you intend to write. Besides, I write an annual marketing plan that utilizes the data you're asking for."

"Sweet. Can I get a copy of that, too."

A long exhale left Tami's lungs as if to signal her reluctance.

"By the way, Tami, do you know the difference between a marketing plan and a market analysis?"

Crickets.

I shot a cocky smirk over to Carla, Tami's secretary, and then marched on with the offensive. "I'll make sure and give you a digital copy of the market analysis once it's complete for you to distribute because you just said how important that is to you. In the meantime, however, take a minute and fish up a copy of your marketing plan and those travel numbers. Thanks for your help. And, Carla, we're going to have a drink sometime soon." Then I left.

Not surprisingly, it took her a week to get me her marketing plan. She handed it to me without saying a word at a Town Board meeting. I have transcribed the cover memo word for word:

> This is the 2005 marketing plan for the Town of [La Blanca Gente]. It is primarily focused on

tourism and bringing people to [La Blanca Gente]. However it does have a large number of facts and figures that are also important for people looking at potentially bring new business or buying an existing business here as well.

If any of these facts and figures are used for or in the development of any other publications or materials to be given to individuals they MUST be referenced as coming from this document. Because they are the property of the Town of [La Blanca Gente], and have taken a great deal of time and effort to get, and some are still difficult to obtain as there is a large amount of education that still needs to take place within our town and business owners as to why facts and figures are important and how they can be helpful to them and us.

There is also a great deal of other collateral information that goes along with this plan that is not necessarily important to outside people and is not generally freely handed out with regard to where we are advertising and why. Because of the inherent competition that we all face when trying to put together the best laid plan to get people to visit [La Blanca Gente] vs. other area towns. While we do work with as many entities as possible to get as much done as possible, some thing still need to be individual.

If you have any questions please feel free to ask, as

I have mentioned I am currently changing this plan for the upcoming year, and many of the number and generalities made within it are no longer valid.

Hmm . . .? She was probably in a hurry to whip out this memo and get it to me by tonight.

Or so I thought, until I started reading the Marketing Plan. I might say, I haven't had a good laugh in a long time and it was extremely satisfying that it came at her expense. But don't take my word for it, take her's. Here is just one tidbit from what turns out to be a thoroughly embarrassing Marketing Plan. In the following paragraph, Tami is attempting to describe where she is advertising and why; at least, I think that's what she is trying to do:

Since 2002 has been on Summer and Winter through small local publications with just one or two with regional or national distribution. However, over the last few years we have begun to target Colorado, New Mexico and Kansas locations, with year round information. Since these are areas with lower visitor numbers but showing a continued interest in our area. We started (in 2002) hitting Denver, Colorado Springs, and Pueblo and Albuquerque Radio and Television News stations with weekly fall color updates and photos, in addition to weather and upcoming events. This effort seems to have help generate more late season travel numbers as we have seen an uncommon increase in sales tax for the season. The increased exposure on the Front Range has increased the overall interest with small rises also noted in New Mexico.

Huh?

If Tami's goal is to confuse and bewilder, she certainly has achieved it. I think it's great, from a personal rivalry standpoint, that Tami writes at a sixth-grade level. However, from a marketing the Town of La Blanca Gente standpoint, it's terrifying. The worst part is that clearly the Town Board does not read the documents that their department heads generate for them to read and, hopefully, use to rest opinions on. It's a sad state of affairs that a woman who does not know the first thing about marketing is in charge of marketing the town. It's an even sadder state of affairs that her bosses have no clue about it.

I wonder what a potential investor ponders after reading through a slue of incomplete sentences, grammatical errors, and misspelled words? Does he think, "Wow! La Blanca Gente is obviously chalk-full of intelligent individuals like me and it is clear the town Marketing Plan is a manifestation of such an occurrence." Or, perhaps, the thought that is running through his head, as it does mine every time I read something of Tami's, is "Where in the name of Virgin Mary did this person learn how to write? I have never witnessed foolishness applied so thoroughly. Why would I invest my money in a marketplace that is instigated by a fool?" It does make me wonder, in all seriousness, how much investment that Marketing Plan has scared away from the town.

Like any good Sicilian, I systematically went through with a red pen and corrected every error I am capable of identifying. For a few moments I felt like that British woman who wrote the book, *Eats, Shoots and Leaves*. My intent, unlike that British author, was not to educate, however. It was to scurry away some proof, i.e., leverage in the event Tami ever felt the need to question my work product. This way, her insultingly unintelligible Marketing Plan, coupled with her superior capability of exercising stupidity, provide me with all the ammo I need in the event she chooses to embark on the path of open war.

What my bosses don't understand is that if you employ amateurs you get amateur results—results seen in their full manifestation via the town Marketing Plan.

There are ways to measure the success of a marketing campaign—cause and effect statistical analysis for starters. What Tami doesn't understand, other than how to market La Blanca Gente, is her wage is directly correlated to the amount of revenue she can bring into town. As it stands now, she only makes upwards of $32,000 a year; pennies, to say the least. Sadly, as it stands now, she's probably over-paid. Lucky for her, collectively, the Town Board is more ignorant than she is when it comes to marketing. More importantly, lucky for her, she's a local like the rest of 'em, which gives her a free pass to get away with producing such idiotic nonsense.

In La Blanca Gente, and this is a symptom of the entire San Luis Valley, one's educational level gives one zero credibility. No, around these here parts, credibility is derived not from the number of books you've read, but from the number of years you've lived in the area. Seeing as I've only been around for about three months, Tami's hand, despite her incompetence, beats mine with aces.

7

Show Me the Money

If the goal of the Town Board is commercial development, the first step toward achieving that end is increasing the population of the town. Since the town only has so much raw land left to develop, increasing potential population densities constitutes a significant consideration. Business development will be severely retarded if we don't decrease set backs and minimum lot sizes. A choice needs to be made, either the town maintains its rural, hodge-podge character by maintaining the current urban design status quo, or we get down to business and lay the groundwork for economic development. You can't have it both ways.

The challenge with La Blanca Gente's Town Board is when I talk the "how to" of urban design and economic development, I may as well be speaking in Latin. The Board of Trustees talk the talk but when it comes down to crunch time a serious case of ambition dysfunction overwhelms all previous notions of bravery. I habitually tell them how to get to the Promise Land; for Christ's sake, I'm pointing the freakin' way, like Saint Peter holding the gates of heaven open, begging them to "come on in." They're just unwilling to walk through it. Another problem is that after now three months of feeding them my most compelling arguments, I've run out of arguments to compel them with.

On every occasion when one attempts to argue a point, there is a certain degree of credibility exposure. For planners, in particular, we don't have a whole lot of credibility to spare, so putting it on the line generally is not a very healthy idea. If you lose too many arguments, one day, you'll end up with no credibility left to lose.

To a certain degree, I can understand the Town Board's apprehension. Periods of transition are difficult for residents and political leaders of any community. Although you can bet that Aspen, Vail, and Telluride have all gone through such transitions. They say they want growth, they say La Blanca Gente needs to change, but stating opinions and acting on opinions are two very different actions.

Therefore, to compensate for the Town Board's lack of action, I've allied myself with the economic development interests of the community in the hopes of stimulating the trustees out of their impotence. Enter the President of the La Blanca Gente Chamber of Commerce and the President of the San Luis Valley Economic Development Council. I've publicly become their advocates, lobbying my bosses on issues that they hold dear to their hearts. It's like a dyslexic version of the old theory of Advocacy Planning because, in this case, I'm advocating for the rich and not the poor.

Planners should not be so concerned with Advocacy Planning per se, but they can exercise their expertise and compassion via sound planning practice. Anthony J. Catanese does have a point. If one wants to be an agent of social change, than perhaps planning is not the proper arena to pursue this change. However, planners should, whenever possible, strive for equity regardless of what the public is perceived to want and regardless if it is contrary to the beliefs of a community. If the community interests do not like the fact that I am trying to stimulate the function of La Blanca Gente, then the community can always terminate me for someone who is more of a tool to their aristocratic whims.

I suspect Norman Krumholz, the patron saint of Advocacy Planning, would be disappointed in me. After all, I am helping rich people. In many cities, planners have the reputation of being doormats to development.

Planners should very much wield our "expert position" as leverage against those who wish to undermine the community vis-à-vis development.

An important point to consider is that planners are not elected officials. Our job is to facilitate the function, rectify problems, and stimulate the economy of a given city, at the sole behest of those that wish to institute such policies. Planners need not toil with what voters might think. In some cases, as in La Blanca Gente's, achieving sound planning involves neglecting the poor. Gentrification is a good example of a policy that, when it works, helps a community at the expense of the poor. Stimulating older, inner city neighborhoods with investment incentives generates economic activity, adds to the economic vigor of a metropolitan core, and, in turn, creates jobs and promotes more investment. The poor who once occupied gentrified neighborhoods are displaced, indeed, but a greater good is achieved in the process.

Planners have traditionally been pitted against developers because developers are not concerned with the greatest good for the greatest number. In fact, in most cases developers are concerned with the smallest good for the smallest number—themselves.

Planners need to express their opinions because, in the arena of city planning, I would think our opinions are valid, despite the groans of pain from city managers and city attorneys. Our job as planners is to make our cities better, rather than following the whims of the incompetent class. If that involves, as Krumholz suggests, setting an agenda, then so be it. Planners need to exercise their position as the "expert" and actively promote the greatest good for the greatest number. Whether this involves a conservative way of doing things a-la gentrification, or a liberal way of doing things a-la challenging developers, it makes no difference what road we take; because, at the end of the day, they all lead to the same place.

Alas, my last best option in La Blanca Gente is to align myself with the ruling class and hope that I can buy the influence necessary to manipulate them toward my way of thinking.

Over the past month, I've been tenaciously working on what has become known as the Town of La Blanca Gente Commercial Market Analysis. I've known for some weeks that Ava and Tami did not appreciate the fact that my time was going into the document, but my bosses gave me the green light to proceed, and proceed I did.

In conjunction with developing the Market Analysis, I started lobbying the Town Board to establish an urban renewal authority (URA). Despite the stigma attached with its name, Colorado URA's have unique powers—tools that the Town Board could exploit. Tax increment financing, for one, allows URA's to collect the difference in property and/or sales taxes before a development is started and after it is completed. If a development, for instance, is a new shopping center constructed on vacant land, such a difference is significant, and can finance millions of dollars in public improvements.

In Colorado, local government entities must ask the voters to finance multi-year commitments; i.e., municipalities have to take every proposed bond package, regardless of whether or not it raises taxes, to the local voters for approval. Colorado URA's are exempt from this state law and can freely pledge their money as they might deem appropriate. This makes URA's a powerful tool in Colorado.

Do I even have to mention that URA's have eminent domain powers?

First things first, though. I need to finish the Market Analysis. Potential developers would routinely walk into Town Hall requesting data that might help them make an informed decision on whether or not to invest in La Blanca Gente. After three months of listening to Ava poison their minds with confusion and speculation, I knew the value of a master data document, something that explained and projected the facts— something that spoke to the untapped real estate capital market, which lies in wait for the next best Colorado resort town to bloom.

When attempting to attract real estate investment to any area, a thorough and all-inclusive market analysis is the first and most important step in the process. Mike E. Miles, et al., states that it is best to look at the macro (market) and micro (individual property) characteristics when formulating a market study.[32] Following their recipe like an evangelical follows the Bible, I meticulously analyzed the supply and demand characteristics for all unit types, absorption rates, and rents and value. I went so far as to actually measure the perimeters of all the commercial units in town in an effort to ascertain square footage, and documented which ones were occupied, which were vacant, and the business sector category for each unit. I asked Ava for all the public data possible regarding annual municipal sales taxes, which was a request Ava begrudged. Then, utilizing the sales tax data, I was able to calculate the average sales per square foot in municipal La Blanca Gente. This was a lot of work, particularly walking the cold, mountain streets, measuring the outside of each building.

La Blanca Gente sales, according to my analysis at least, average roughly $168 per square foot.[33] Perhaps the most sought after number in my entire 29 page document did not even warrant a battered eyelash when I shared the information with my bosses. A testament to their ignorance, they wouldn't know a good market analysis if it slapped them across the face.

My analysis was developing into a beast of burden. With half a dozen painstaking projections, a wealth of data collection, and months of work, no stone was left unturned.

A rural market by any definition, the most difficult part about convincing developers to invest in La Blanca Gente would be developing a sound argument that the trade area has the potential to produce returns. The International Council of Shopping Centers (ICSC), the commercial development industry's primary professional organization, is not shy about sharing the tricks of the trade in an effort to help communities attract more development. Perhaps the best manual for giving small communities direction is the ICSC's *Developing Successful Retail in Secondary and Rural*

Markets. At only 72 pages, chalk full of pictures and maps, the book looks like it was printed at Kinko's, but the information contained therein provides keen insights in precisely what national retailers are examining when considering new markets.

ICSC's step one includes defining a given market's trade area: "Defining a retail trade area is an art and a science. In general, a trade area should reflect the geography from which 75 [to] 90 percent of retail sales are generated."[34]

Indeed, defining La Blanca Gente's trade area will be an art and a science. The two largest businesses in town are a general store and a hardware store, which serve the passer-by and La Blanca Gente's immediate population. Otherwise, there are a couple of gas stations, a couple of liquor stores, a couple of bars, and a few restaurants.

The lowest point in La Blanca Gente's market cycle is no doubt January and February. A virtual ghost town, all the seasonal home owners have vacated the area for warmer climes; the RV parks are empty, and lodging facilities only have a handful of rooms occupied. I've heard stories of how, once upon a time, there were only two or three families that stayed in town over the winter months to weather the conditions.

With the Village at Wolf Creek looming on the horizon, the La Blanca Gente commercial real estate market seems poised to enter a phase of expansion, which will no doubt attract a large cohort of upper-income spenders. Being only shouting distance from the Village at Wolf Creek, it is safe to assume many travelers to the ski area will wish to explore neighboring communities. Likewise, for those who may not be able to afford to stay at the Village, La Blanca Gente will likely be their alternative overnight destination. Furthermore, as construction begins at the Village, La Blanca Gente will provide the services, both personal and project related, to the large number of construction workers needed to complete the project. The Village at Wolf Creek, in short, will provide the winter time business opportunities that are currently unsustainable in La

Blanca Gente and a cause for many start-up businesses to shutter their doors.

By summer, however, the region hums with activity. The Texans come back, recreationalists from the Front Range explore the area, the RV parks are full of those who can't afford seasonal homes, and lodging occupancy rates hover around 80 percent. Like wet season on the Serengeti, summer in La Blanca Gente provides for all.

There is little uncertainty, however, that the economic capital of the San Luis Valley is Alamosa, Colorado, which serves roughly 50,000 people. Folks from all over the Valley drive to Alamosa for their routine needs. True to form, me and/or my lovely wife make the trip at least once per week. The nested economy of Alamosa feeds into the nested economy of Pueblo, Colorado, which then feeds into Denver, and Denver then feeds into New York City, at which point the money starts the long cycle back down to La Blanca Gente in the form of rich white people buying seasonal homes and local goods to support them.

A true testament to the merits of Central Place Theory, and, not to mention, the theory as propagated by Neal R. Peirce, et al., and William R. Dodge in books such as *Citi States* and *Regional Excellence*, that direct economic regions should band together and act cohesively in an effort to compete in today's global economy. Alamosa is almost literally smack-dab in the geographic center of the Valley. From La Blanca Gente, Alamosa is an hour away. Therefore, new retail in La Blanca Gente needs to recapture the lost sales tax dollar that migrates from La Blanca Gente to Alamosa, as well as be unique enough to attract those who live up to half way between La Blanca Gente and Alamosa to provide for the potential of capturing their dollar.

Between the Village at Wolf Creek, the elitist Ty Webb Club, and potential retail recapture, La Blanca Gente ought to be in a position to attract small-market national retail chains. Walgreen's, Starbucks, a decent sized grocery store, and your typical mix of strip mall tenants, are all within La Blanca Gente's grasp, but no one's ever reached out to take it. Everyone is aware, and rightfully so, that in all likelihood, in order to attract commercial investments, the La Blanca Gente Town Board will need to pony a few bucks in incentives. And there is no money, right?

Don't be scared; Papa Tedesco will hold you and tell you everything is going to be all right. I'll lightly stroke the tears from your cheek, caress your hair, and even hold your hand. It's so simple: all one needs is to establish a new and stable revenue stream that can finance the construction of public improvements. I'll get to that later. For now, the point is that there is a large gulf in knowledge between identifying what a quality project is and actually financing such a project. Councils, planners, and bureaucrats in general don't know how to close a deal. If a planner can establish a predictable revenue stream for a given project, though, the battle has been won. That's the point where a planner tells their council that, "If you want this deal to happen, it's time to pull in a financial advisor and bond counselor. Otherwise, this deal dies." And that's all there is to it. Since the financial advisor and bond counsel get paid when a deal closes, they are sufficiently motivated to shepherd you and your council to get to a closing and disbursement of funds.

The trick is stimulating the market to take action now rather than later, which brings us back to my reference to creating an urban renewal authority and establishing a revenue stream to pay for some goodies. Don't get caught up in the stigma that the name invokes. Throughout the 1950s and 60s the Fed's subsidized local urban renewal programs for slum clearance, blight removal, and subsequent redevelopment. This is the era when URA's made a name for themselves by demolishing pleasant, livable, and reasonably safe neighborhoods—communities that displayed many of the key facets of contemporary urban theory in regard to smart growth—whose only fault was being populated by minority, low income residents. During this era, the term minority encompassed some European ethnicities, as well. Sadly, the neighborhoods were replaced with cold, lifeless urban landscapes, a simple expressway, or both. When Nixon axed Fed funds for local urban renewal projects, many local urban renewal authorities disappeared. However, suffice to say, urban renewal's reputation was made.

It would please many to know, at least in the world of government driven economic development, that the drivers of such discourse have learned from their mistakes. Thanks in large part to Herbert Gans and Jane Jacobs correctly identifying the independent relationship between blight and poverty, today's economic development planners understand that it's okay to be poor, and poor neighborhoods are okay, too, so long as they're pleasant and livable.

Understanding that each and every state has differing urban renewal legislation, policy makers needed to identify a local source of funding to continue urban renewal efforts in the post Nixon era. In Colorado's case, it's tax increment financing (TIF). Dreamed up in the Communist Republic of California in the 1950s, whoever was the first to coin the idea of tax increment financing deserves a Noble Prize in Economics. Generally speaking, utilizing the tax increment is a simple process of circling an area and deeming said area a tax increment district. In Colorado, once an area is formally identified and adopted, it has statutory claim to all the incremental property taxes generated from it, not just the property taxes generated by virtue of the municipal mill levy but all mills taxed vis-à-vis all local entities. The difference between TIF funds and Federal grants is TIF is a market driven revenue stream and Fed grants are not, which means the application of TIF funds for urban renewal projects must be much more calculated due to the inherent risk of any given project.

A carryover that survived the years between Federally funded urban renewal authorities and today's locally funded authorities is the term "blight;" i.e., there must be a nexus between an urban renewal project and blight removal. "Blight" is a term more understood by reputation than by legal definition. Blight's reputation being born in the 1950s and 60s and blight's legal definition being born within Colorado State Statues. By reputation, blight is also associated with low income neighborhoods, though blight need not equal low income. A low income household, and/or a cluster of them, is not blight. Blight factors are those forces that inhibit the real estate market from optimal functionality. In the case of an urban renewal area in La Blanca Gente, blight is a simple lack of infrastructure. Thus, the entirety of the municipality could be deemed blighted.

There are those that make a bad habit of criticizing the use of tax increment financing. Their simplified argument being, "You're stealing property tax growth from the other taxing entities." Naturally, those whom levy such an argument typically represent counties and school districts. The better read among them may even cite what is commonly called "The Chicago Study." Written by the Developing Neighborhood Alternatives Project and published by the conservative Heartland Institute in a 2003 edition of *Policy Studies*, "The Right Tool for the Job: an Analysis of Tax Increment Financing," is now gospel for the anti-TIF zealots. There is indeed some contradiction to be found in the Heartland Institute's willingness to underwrite such a study given that TIF is the most market driven solution for governments to employ in an effort to cure market failures. Not to mention, TIF does not raise taxes.

The study analyzes five Chicago area tax increment districts and quantifies their impacts on their respective neighborhoods and the city as a whole. The conclusions drawn by the authors of the study are sweeping. Their hypothesis is equally aggressive, stating: "This report analyzes who benefits from TIF, who pays for those benefits, and whether TIF promotes or hinders justice and fairness in the community."[35]

To put the Chicago Study in perspective, those who begrudge TIF with declarations of community harm, including the authors of the Chicago Study, rest their arguments on five TIF districts within a city that, as of 2006, has 142 TIF districts.[36] The authors of the Chicago Study do not mention how many TIF districts were in Chicago during the analysis period (2003). They do mention, however, that, ". . . the five selected TIF districts represent a small percentage of the existing districts in the city of Chicago . . ."[37] To make matters worse, the authors apply their largely negative conclusions uniformly to all TIF districts throughout the country.

Five TIF districts in a city that consists of many dozens is not a statistically significant sample—in no way does it represent the average impact of any given TIF district on a given neighborhood or community. To make matters statistically worse, "The [authors] chose which TIF districts would be evaluated and what data would be gathered."[38] This is to say, the five TIF districts analyzed were not even a random sample. One could, without a whole lot of effort, build a case that the authors came into the study with an already developed bias against TIF and cherry-picked five of the worst performing Chicago area tax increment districts as crucibles for their pre-conceived notions. But I digress.

Today's urban renewal programs are not the same as the experiences of Herbert Gans in Boston's West End or Jane Jacobs duking it out with Robert Moses. In La Blanca Gente, a town with no property tax, a town that solely survives on sales tax and the insignificant revenue generated from court fees, speeding tickets, and other miscellaneous fees; utilizing an URA for the property tax increment would allow the town to collect the growth in property tax assessments currently levied within municipal boundaries by other taxing entities. Simply put: by establishing an URA, La Blanca Gente could utilize growth in property tax revenue from their mother county, the water district, and the school district. And, yes, it would all be in the name of blight removal.

Arguments regarding whether the utilization of TIF is "right" or "wrong" are not relevant. The proper argument is whether or not the town would like to control its own destiny. In municipal planning, money equates to leverage. He who hands out the money is he who calls the shots. Developers will happily do whatever you ask them to do if it means government is going to finance their public improvements. Otherwise, they'll just develop to the minimum standards as outlined in the land use code, which, in most cases, is totally inadequate. Because administrators at the county, the school district, and the water district are not well versed within the realm of government-driven economic development, adoption of an URA would fly right under their radar. A stealth maneuver, it would be two or three years before they would fully understand what hit them.

Such a notion is a stroke of genius, really, because the town is broke, and residents would absolutely refuse to institute a new property tax on themselves. Establishing an URA skips all the usual political nonsense— like a ballot question—and the Board of Trustees could generate a windfall without even having to hold an election. The county, the water district, and the school district may raise a fuss, but the natural argument is that they still maintain their buying power, we're just banking on the future tax growth to invest in new growth.

In La Blanca Gente's case, identifying an URA project (TIF) area would turn on a money spigot. Cold hard cash that may be spent without a vote of the people on whatever the URA board might deem appropriate.

Because URA's do not cash-flow, i.e., produce tax revenue after the first year or two of formation, the theoretical La Blanca Gente URA could sign reimbursement deals with developers, essentially stating, "you front your own incentives, and we'll pay you back as the tax increment flows over time." Such a strategy takes all of the risk off La Blanca Gente and places the risk solely where risk should be placed: the private sector.

Typically, developers will push back at the "reimbursement over time" concept likely with an argument of "we don't have the equity to purchase our incentives up-front." A simple conversation with their lenders and/or investors is usually enough for the developer's moneyed interests to increase the credit capacity for the deal. Because the tax increment is, generally speaking, all the property taxes generated from new taxable property improvements, the open market sets the limit for how many reimbursement deals an URA could potentially cut.

The downside with reimbursement deals is the public improvements (and the accompanying private developments) are piecemeal in nature. They happen one at a time independent of each other. Therefore, there may be times, if you're indeed looking for everything to happen at once, where it is a good idea to invest the tax increment into some revenue bonds and underwrite a catalyst project with the proceeds. Revenue bonds differ from general obligation bonds in that the tax payers are not on the hook to cover the debt service should their mother government find themselves short on the revenue pledged to repay the bonds. No, revenue bonds are repaid solely on the revenue generated from the deal that they are financing.

Considering the fact that La Blanca Gente is absent a central business district, buying ourselves a "downtown" with some revenue bonds appears to be the most appropriate course of action.

I pitched the idea of establishing an URA via a Power Point presentation during a Town Board work session. Knowing full well that I needed outside support, I invited the President of the San Luis Valley Economic Development Council and the President of the La Blanca Gente Chamber of Commerce to join me. Naturally, the Town Board, Ava, Tami, and one of the town attorneys were also present during the meeting.

When I concluded my ten-minute presentation, a voice from the gallery chimed up in support, "Guys, this is just the type of new ideas needed to help this town grow. I'm in full support." I looked up and smiled as Grady Ryan, the San Luis Valley Economic Development Council President, voiced his support. Grady is a man of charisma and confidence, and his opinions always demand respect. He is one who made a bundle of money in the private sector and, since then, was one of the first middle-aged, upper middle class, white people to live permanently in La Blanca Gente. Grady, despite his right-wing demeanor, is a total stud and one who drives change in the region.

The Town Board spent five minutes discussing my proposed concept. They were well aware that it would be a political process to actually establish an urban renewal authority and then adopt a project area. I told them, "There's no need to give me direction at this very moment. I'll give everyone a couple of weeks before I bring the topic up again."

That night I bought Grady and his compatriot, Dalton Roads—the President of the La Blanca Gente Chamber of Commerce—both a beer and thanked them for supporting me during the meeting. While we sat in the tavern nearest to La Blanca Gente Town Hall, Ava and Tami came strutting in to partake in a nightcap as well. Pretending not to notice us as they walked past our table, they sat at the bar with their backs to our conversation. "Those two really know how to get in my way," I said with my beer bottle poised at my lips simultaneously shaking my head.

"I'm with ya, Tedesco," was Grady's response. Grady then called the waitress to the table and directed her to put the next round of drinks for Ava and Tami on his tab. "Keep your friends close and your enemies closer," Grady said to me with a smile as the waitress left the table.

Several weeks passed as I followed the normal work routine—writing the Market Analysis and processing whatever land use nonsense came my way to process.

Finally, about a month later, at the town's regular Board of Trustees meeting, I decided it was time to push the URA question again. It was the usual routine at the Town Board meeting, not a lot of big, controversial decisions, just the usual mundane, day-to-day bullshit. The Town Board has an uncanny ability, however, to turn small decisions into an inquisition.

Toward the end of the meeting, during the "Operations Reports" portion of the agenda, the mayor called upon me and said, "Mike, what have you been up to over the past month?" I gave them my usual lines: processing subdivisions, writing the Market Analysis, and "just trying to stay out of trouble."

"Good to hear, Mike. Anything else?"

"Yes, actually, I approached the seven of you about a month ago proposing that we embark down the road of establishing an urban renewal authority. Would you like me to proceed with that concept?"

For just a moment, the room was silent. Then, out of nowhere, the town attorney chimed up and said, "Ya know, there are a lot of options available to Colorado municipalities within the realm of economic development. There are business improvements districts, downtown development authorities, metropolitan districts, whatever you prefer."

I sat there in a state of shock, knowing full well the attorney just killed my idea. He wasn't even at the work session when I pitched it, his side-kick was, and now he's chiming up adding to the general state of confusion, making the question more complex.

"Maybe we should look into all the options available to us?" The mayor said in the direction of his six colleagues. Without even wincing an eye-lash, they all agreed with him.

"Mike, keep looking into what options we have and we'll talk in the future." The mayor then turned to Tami and the conversation with me was over.

I looked at Rusty, the town attorney who killed my idea, with a fire in my belly normally reserved for Ava and Tami. He wasn't being malicious toward me; he just opened his mouth without any context to that which he was speaking. He should know better than to give people options, particularly city councils. Options can be used as excuses, and now the La Blanca Gente Town Board had all the excuses they needed to kick the can down the road and prolong an actual decision. The time for La Blanca Gente to consider options has passed. It is time for action, and Rusty just inadvertently stamped out my best hope for stimulating action.

The attorneys for the Town of La Blanca Gente are like all La Blanca Gente town staff: overworked and underpaid. Old and young, one beginning his career, the other in his twilight, Tony and Rusty are the only other two trained professionals the Town of La Blanca Gente has on the payroll. Naturally, I learned to like them quite quickly. Rusty Senex, legal partner in a one-man partnership dubbed Senex Law, represents most every town in the San Luis Valley. Tony, the young one, is a stud by nature. Rusty hired Tony to help handle the workload. I tend to call or email one of them at least once or twice a day. I can tell Rusty is wondering why I know so little in the way of general municipal rules and procedures. He has said to me on occasion, "Didn't you learn this in school?" And I would always reply, "Well, no Rusty, they don't teach the requirements of the La Blanca Gente Land Use Code and the Colorado Revised Statutes in the Urban Planning Department at the University of Kansas, but thanks for making me feel like a dip shit."

It was Tony, like a hound-dog, that was the first to sense that Ava and I were not getting along. "How are things going with Ava," he would say. And I would respond, "Everyday we're another step closer to World War III."

Since the Town Board wanted options, I went to work organizing a series of memos outlining special districts in Colorado and the differences between them. They're all basically the same, though, and I knew it would be months before I could get them back into the position I had them before the town attorney thought it best to give planning advice rather than legal advice. And thus, La Blanca Gente's development horizon is still out of reach.

8

Escape

Dad and I have developed a routine that I am quite pleased with whenever I make the three and a half hour trip up to Denver. Pop is your classic baby-boomer: divorced, living in a big city, lots of disposable income, and just looking to have a good time. He's paid his dues raising a family of five kids, working two, three jobs at a time, living on food stamps and paycheck to paycheck.

Pop knows all the great haunts in Denver. Every nook and cranny, every hole in the wall, every eccentric restaurant. He knows where they are and he knows whether or not they're worth a damn. He's on a first name basis with many of the house bands that play around downtown Denver. The bartenders throughout downtown, however, know him not by name but by drink—Sapphire martini strait-up, three olives. He'll show up at swing-dance clubs and all the ladies know his name and want to dance with him. With a wallet full of money and a lifetime of sacrifice behind him, there's nothing left to do but have a good time. Pop is Mr. Denver.

We always start the day by meeting my brother Paul, yet another man of fine Sicilian stock, at our favorite 9-hole executive golf course, at which point Mr. Denver beats us both at a round of golf. Then, inevitably, we all go home to take naps. When we awake, we make the trip to Mikey's Italian Bistro in the Highlands neighborhood of Denver proper. Enjoying what is perhaps the best damn food in Denver, we let the cabernet flow liberally, and I always enjoy the New York Steak. Slathered with mushrooms in a fine garlic sauce, who wouldn't enjoy that steak? Mikey's is your quintessential neighborhood Italian joint: cozy, with pictures of Sinatra hanging on the wall swaying mostly to Sinatra softly playing in the background. After dinner, feeling as though men of our class stratification do not deserve to be physically and emotionally satisfied to such a degree, we adjourn to a cigarette in Mikey's parking lot. It's at this point in the evening I get my first creeping suspicions that a guy like me is meant to be in a big city like Denver—drinking good drink and eating good eats.

Also, this is the point in the evening where Paul's domestication catches up with him. It's not that he does not want to come out and hit the town with Mr. Denver and I. It's just that the poor bastard is so accustomed to falling asleep around 8:30 or 9:00 that his motivation to have a good time diminishes exponentially once the clock strikes 8:00. I kiss Paul's kids, hug his wife, hug Paul, and that's that—not to be seen until the next time I come around Denver.

Mr. Denver and I enjoy another cigarette in Mikey's parking lot and plot our next move. I look around the neighborhood. Behind Mikey's are tree lined streets, sidewalks, houses that all share the same architectural genre, yet are all different. In front and parallel to Mikey's are commercial and apartment buildings. The warm air is sweetened by the everyday pollutants of a big city: ozone, carbon emissions, dust, particulates. Heaven. It's a freakin' neighborhood, so much so that looking around it gives me a sense of nostalgia for the damn place.

Mr. Denver and I decide to head into lower downtown Denver— "Lodo"—to a dive jazz joint called *El Chapultepec*. The jazz gods smile upon *El Chapultepec*. It's my kind of place: inconspicuous, not infested with pop-culture posers, a dive by any definition, and right on the outskirts of the 5-Points neighborhood of Denver, i.e., the hood. Mr. Denver and I walk into *El Chapultepec* feeling real good, so much so that everyone in the joint can notice the Sicilian in our struts. The smoke-filled air fills our nostrils like roses in bloom on a Sunday morning. It's packed; nowhere to sit, so we stand. My eye wanders to the young ladies throughout the room who make me question my fidelity. We manage to simultaneously order our drinks while we light our cigarettes—Sapphire martini for Mr. Denver and the house cabernet for me. Mr. Denver is only a recreational smoker, perhaps only smoking a pack every two weeks. In places like *El Chapultepec*, however, smoking is a pre-requisite upon entrance. I, however, have been addicted since I was 12—the fruits of growing up in a low-income neighborhood in Spokane.

El Chapultepec features a house band that practices the theory of less is more. Although, perhaps it's because of environmental factors that the owners of *El Chapultepec* cannot field more than a drummer, bassist, pianist, and the occasional horn player because their stage is no more than 20 square feet. No matter; the audience is on top of the band and the band is on top of the audience; they wouldn't have it any other way.

Mr. Denver and I puff our cigarettes, drink our drinks, and enjoy the music.

We finally spot an open seat and like a fox on a mouse, we pounce. The band takes a break, which gives Mr. Denver and me an opportunity to talk. Naturally, we start talking about jazz. We start with Duke Ellington, work our way through Charles Mingus, bad mouth Buddy Rich for being too flashy, and finish with Tito Puente. We chuckle at the injustice that most of the old jazz gods from the John Coltrane/Miles Davis glory days are either in Europe scratching out a living, living a life of elderly poverty in the States, or dead.

Mr. Denver and I enjoy the atmosphere, smoking our smokes, drinking our drinks, chatting with random drunkards, and drinking a couple more drinks. Never satisfied, however, our minds feel the urge to ramble on. Like clockwork, we decide to walk a few blocks over to *Eno Tica*, an up-scale jazz joint with a full restaurant and cigar room.

On a warm Denver summer night there is nothing like walking

around downtown: the people on the streets, half naked women, the sites, sounds, and smells. It is times like these where I feel one with life. I refrain from smoking on the walk over so I can drink-in the air, stare at the street trees flowing in the breeze, and give my body and mind a chance to reintroduce themselves. Like Edward Abbey by himself in the middle of a desert, bar hopping on a warm summer night is my spiritual escape.

Mr. Denver and I find our way to *Eno Tica*. Inside it's dark, mellow, round black tables surrounded by three black chairs pepper the room. A bluegrass band is playing softly on the stage. To my satisfaction, they are playing at a decibel where people are still able to have conversations without screaming across the table at one another.

We find a table; I look at my watch: 11:30. Hmm, getting late. Better have another smoke and order a drink. Mr. Denver, likely hitting his tolerance, orders a beer rather than his usual Sapphire martini. I ask the waitress if she has an IPA floating around. She says no, so I order the house cab.

No doubt feeling motivated from the five or six glasses of wine coursing through my blood stream, I feel compelled to start telling Mr. Denver about all the shit I pulled as a teenager. I tell him about all the dope I used to smoke in my bedroom, about the parties I threw while he was away and about the neighbors I pissed off as a result. Dad nods and smiles. Then I got into the heavy stuff.

I told him about a drunken drive home when I was fifteen, my best friend's older brother driving a car that his dad had spent all summer fixing up for him. We're driving through downtown Spokane after a long night of drinking in the woods. The streets are empty—no surprise for Spokane. We spot three or four large black garbage bags peppering the road. From the back seats, my best friend and I start yelling, "HIT 'EM, HIT 'EM!" The driver's best friend, from shotgun, yells, "DON'T HIT 'EM, DON'T HIT 'EM!" Obviously a bit torn as to what action should be taken, the driver heads straight toward the bags, then, at the last moment, thinks twice about hitting them and swerves sharply to avoid them. Swerves, that is, sharply into an oncoming telephone pole. We hit it dead-on.

Everyone staggers out of the car and the four of us look at each other. In an instant, the friend who was sitting shotgun darts off and vanishes. Clearly, as my best friend and I look at each other, there is an important decision to be made: run and leave the driver to his own devices—underage, drunk, with bottles of vodka in the back seat—or stay and take the heat with him. Naturally, we ran like hell out of there. Lucky for us the sprint back to my house was only thirteen or fourteen blocks. We could hear sirens in the distance as we cut through private properties to avoid the lights of the street. We made it back to my dad's apartment, rested for a moment, and then adjourned for a cigarette out on the balcony.

Mr. Denver, sipping his beer, nods and laughs. I can't quite tell if he's just being polite or if he really thinks my story is humorous. We order another round of drinks and light another round of cigarettes. The night is starting to catch up with us. We order some appetizers off the menu: smoked salmon bruschetta, garlic shrimp, stuffed mushrooms—sure beats French Toast at Denny's on the way home.

The food comes and we nourish our souls. Feeling a second wind, I decide to tell Dad about the time when I was in the eighth grade and the Geography Bee came through my junior high school.

The initial Geography Bee test was to be given in social studies class and as luck would have it, I happened to show up that day. There were just over 20 students in the classroom waiting to take the test. I sat in my usual seat in the very back row at the end of the aisle (so I would not disturb anyone when I got up to take my customary mid-hour bathroom break). Next to me was the quintessential class nerd—a tall, lanky, odd-looking boy with glasses who always seemed to have a pen handy. The teacher passed out the tests, which consisted of 10 multiple-choice questions. As I took the test I was amazed at how simple it was. In what country is the city of London located? Or: The state of Hawaii is located in what ocean? And:

Which of the following cities is most likely to be a port? I was astonished! I finished the test and looked up to discover I was the first one done. When everyone in class was finished the teacher collected the papers and then handed them out again, making sure no student got their own exam so we could correct the test as a class. After correcting the papers we handed them back to their owners, my girl got a six out of ten—what a fool. As I expected, my test was perfect and I sat back in my chair feeling quite proud.

My instructor needed to know how we all did so the top student could advance to the next round of the Geography Bee. We were all to announce our scores out loud, one-at-a-time, starting in the front of class and ending with yours truly, Mr. Ten Out of Ten. The students started to round off their scores, "six out of ten," "four out of ten," "seven out of ten," "three out of ten," I was dumb-founded. Was I surrounded by idiots? "Five out of ten," "three out of ten," I could not believe what I was hearing. Could this be possible? It was almost my turn and at this time I knew I was going to get the only ten out of ten in the class. "Five out of ten," "four out of ten," Just the nerd, then it's my turn. I couldn't wait to see the look on my teacher's face when me, the class hoodlum, announced his, "ten out of ten." What? The nerd got a ten out of ten? I thought I was going to start crying. That was my ten out of ten. "Mike." I looked up. "It's your turn," announced the teacher. "Um . . . ten out of ten," I said not too confidently. My teacher didn't buy it. She thought I copied from the nerd and there was no arguing with her. There was nothing I could do but boycott school for the next few days. In the end, the nerd won Geography Champion of the entire school, got a trophy and his face put in the yearbook. To this day I'm bitter. Should-of-been my face in the fucking yearbook.

Mr. Denver smiled at this anecdote, lit another smoke, and ordered what is likely his last drink. I do the same in succession. Twelve forty-five AM. Where does the time go? We even out the tab (i.e., Dad pays the bill) and embark on one last walk through downtown Denver to the car for the ride home. Mr. Denver is probably a DUI waiting to happen, but the less said about that the better.

On the way back to Lakewood, where Dad's condo is, we spot on the horizon a cluster of flashing lights—police lights. "What's that?" Mr. Denver said glancing over at me. "Looks like the police," I reply. "Unless you want to deal with what might be a sobriety check-point, I suggest you hang a left turn as soon as possible."

Dad turns on his blinker and mumbles incoherently to the driver's side window. Not the most subtle of evasive maneuvers considering, at this point, we were only a block away from the lights; but, as the seconds ticked by and we realized more and more that we probably just avoided a night in jail, we managed to swerve the rest of the way home without interruption.

9

Politics

It's now November in the Colorado Rockies. The Aspens and Cottonwoods have shed their leaves but La Blanca Gente has yet to get its first big snow storm. I've not grown accustom to the 60 degree room temperature of the Colorado High Country; perpetually chilly, I've also yet to learn to wear layers throughout the day and shed what's not needed.

Ava handed me a memo a week earlier requesting that all department heads organize their proposed 2006 budgets. I already knew that there is no money in the budget for the big frills, but there is some wiggle room for small perks. Naturally, I placed a few said perks into my budget. Aside from my 2006 salary, which I figured at $35,124, and some office supplies, I plugged in three conferences and a membership in the American Planning Association (APA). I prepared myself for the pushback on the conferences. I suspected that Ava wasn't going to let that shit through unscathed. The conferences, with travel and lodging, added up to roughly $4,000. Two conferences are sponsored by the APA for continuing education while the third, hosted by the International Council of Shopping Centers, provided an avenue for economic development. Thus, my budget—the Town of La Blanca Gente Planning Department's budget—totaled roughly $44,000 when I finished.

Forty-four thousand dollars of a $630,000 budget, the lowest of all departments. That's about seven percent of the budget in a town that only has four departments. A pittance. The tragedy was I knew I would have to scrap for every cent. The Marketing Director's budget came out to roughly $76,000; police protection totaled about $173,000, while Ava somehow managed the remainder. One does not have to be a professional planner to know that the urban ills of La Blanca Gente are a consequence of non-planning. Thus, already woefully under-funded, I prepared myself for the shit-storm of defending three freakin' conferences and a lousy membership in the American Planning Association.

The whole situation agitated me. On the cusp of having a woman with a high-school diploma attack my budget because I budgeted funding for continuing education is a poetic injustice. Ava would be well served to attend a seminar or two herself; perhaps then her mind would open from the narrows of complete and utter ignorance and she would then see a world far wider than La Blanca Gente. Whatever; if it's a fight she wants, it's a fight she'll get.

The Town Board agreed on a work session to grind out the budget a couple nights after they were handed a draft budget in early November. The night of the work session, like clockwork, the only people to show up to the meeting were the mayor, because he's retired and has nothing better to do, his wife, because she follows the mayor around like a lost puppy, and all of the town department heads. A complete and utter waste of time. With no quorum of trustees, official decisions could not be made.

We sat, the mayor, his wife, me, Ava, Tami, and the police chief, and talked about nothing for a couple of hours before the mayor, finally, decided to take a look at the budget. Uncomfortably, the discussion migrated toward my proposed budget. I had placed a relatively sizable contingency into my budget in the hopes of utilizing it for pet projects I had been discussing with local civic organizations, not the least of which being new entry way signs into the town. I could not, however, let on that the intent of the contingency was for such improvements because it was not the time to fight such a battle. My soon to be erroneous assumption was that if I place a high contingency into my budget, then they would trim the fat off that bone and not touch the stuff I really thought was appropriate.

In the end, I willfully, under the assumption that making token concessions now will make it easier to argue what I need in the next work session, gave up roughly $5,000 from my budget. This, along side other minor concessions here and there throughout the entire town budget, put it at $30,000 from being balanced.

The next discussion regarding the 2006 Town of La Blanca Gente budget happened at the end of a regular monthly meeting of the Town Board. Luckily for me, it was already a long night—annexing some land and adopting the new and quite hapless Town of La Blanca Gente Land Use Code—it was 11:00 PM when we got around to the budget. Earlier in the evening I spotted in the "revenues" section of the budget a gross under-estimation of what Ava conceived the Planning Department would pull in from developer fees. I pointed this out to the Town Board, and they agreed that my department would generate more revenue than what Ava had initially "projected." For the time being, the budget was balanced. The rub, however, came when a few Town Board members chimed up and suggested one more work session to finalize the budget and give them an opportunity to actually take a look at the damn thing.

A couple days later I again found myself in the Town Hall conference room to chat with my bosses about the budget. This time, however, five of them managed to show up. Tami was absent due to one of her mysterious trade shows, which are, evidently, a pivotal component of her annual "Marketing Plan."

The Town Board spent a lot of time allowing the police chief to explain the reasoning behind his budget; they were very receptive to his arguments. From time to time, though, the mayor would initiate side conversations with his colleagues on the Town Board lobbying them against the conferences I had put in my budget. Naturally, it was easy for me to overhear this. My adrenaline began to pump just a bit as I prepared to battle over the perks I placed in my budget.

When it came time to tackle my budget, the mayor got to the point: "Mike, I don't think there is a need for you to go to these three conferences. If you go to any conference, it should be the one in Telluride because it's the closest." The mayor's colleagues on the Town Board said nothing and it was clear they were waiting for my response.

"Why's that?" I asked.

The Mayor of La Blanca Gente—Pete Balbutio—is a career Kentucky Department of Transportation employee and chose La Blanca Gente as a nice place to retire. Pushing 70 and half bald, Pete is at just about every meeting I attend as they relate to economic development. I get the feeling that it's not because he cares about what happens in La Blanca Gente per se, more because it's just a hobby for him, something to keep his mind occupied.

"Well," Pete said in his usual stammer, "I don't think it will be politically feasible for you to head out of state."

The Town Board was silent.

"Politically feasible to head out of state?" I said. "The politics in this town amount to nothing more than the old-timers gossiping at the gas station over a cup of truck-stop coffee. It's not like we're fighting the press and spinning our message. For Christ's sake, the town's spin machine can't spin her way out of the Visitors' Center."

A couple of chuckles from the Town Board solidified my confidence.

I continued: "Look guys, you have four administrative staff employed for the town—a Planning Director, a Marketing Director, a Town Clerk, and the Chief of Police. I'll let the others speak for themselves but I'm interested in keeping track of the trends in my field."

What I've noticed about Pete over the past five months is that every opinion he expresses on the Town Board is always justified by the statement, "Well, in KDOT this is what we used to do so I think we should do it this way." Simply, Pete's entire perception of the universe is predicated on the work he did and the policies that were carried out by a dysfunctional state transportation department.

"Can you explain the conferences, Mike." Pete said.

"I would love to. The first conference is in San Antonio and is underwritten by the American Planning Association. There's some networking opportunities but, by and large, it's mostly educational. The conference in Denver is also educational and is focused on land use policies. Finally, the conference that I am keenly interested in is the ICSC's annual conference in Las Vegas. This is the Big Kahuna."

"Why's that?" Pete asked.

"Good question, Pete. This conference is every developer, retail corporation, restaurant corporation, and lending institutions' annual trip to Mecca. This is where they go to pray to the Gods of Real Estate Development. This is where deals get made. This is where the private sector goes to create business opportunities, and it works. Five times a day everyone looks east and another opportunity falls in your lap. Roughly 50,000 old white guys walking up and down the Las Vegas Convention Center with a wallet full of credit hunting for untapped markets. La Blanca Gente could be that market. If this board is interested in swimming in tax revenues, this is the conference to send me to."

The Town Board members sat silent for a moment. I felt a pump of adrenaline in anticipation of their response. The mayor chimed up, "Well, Mike, your job isn't really to do economic development."

His statement hit me in the gut and knocked the wind out of me. When I was in the 7th grade at a Catholic school in Spokane, I got beat-up by a public school 7th grader just because he thought I was one of the rich kids. Too terrified and confused to put up a fight, I let him hit me a couple of times before I finally gathered the courage to run away.

Equally as terrified and confused, my heart sank at the sound of Pete's statement. If my job isn't economic development, then what the hell am I doing here? Has it all been a waste of time?

Shocked, I felt the anger brew inside of me like a pot of water coming to a boil, and I said, "If I'm not doing it, then who is?" Pete didn't have an answer to such a profound question. In the few moments that followed my mind darted back to the two interviews I had with the Town Board prior to employment where they stated repeatedly, "We need development, we need the tax revenue." To which I said, "No problem, gentlemen."

My mind shifted to preparing itself for the next volley. Naturally, Ava threw it: "Tami's job is economic development."

"I'm under the impression that Tami strictly operates under a promotional capacity for the town," I said. I expected another Town Board member to back me up on this point because in a previous conversation he expressed the same opinion to me. He didn't back me up, though, the son-of-a-bitch. He sat there mute, like the prick that he is.

"No," Ava said, "Tami is the one who works on economic development."

"Well, if that's the case," I said, "what kind of development specifically is she working on? I still don't know, exactly, what it is that Tami does."

Ava responded: "Mike, if you don't know by now, you're not paying attention. She markets the town."

"I am perhaps the only one who is paying attention, Ava. Which is why I have all these questions. How is she 'marketing the town,' as you say, and how does that relate to economic development?"

"Mike, you're supposedly an educated guy. Marketing the town brings more tourists and more tourists means more sales tax revenue. Didn't you read that in a book at school?" Ava said.

"Ava, I've read more books in a semester than what you'll read in a lifetime. I don't appreciate any suggestion, particularly coming from you, 'Miss High School Diploma,' regarding what I know and what I don't know.

Furthermore, you're on some pretty wobbly ground casting judgment on who it is that has the expertise to do what. Therefore, let me clarify it for you. I know that Tami has the writing skills of a sixth grader. I know that you're terrified of change because it would translate to a life that you don't have the social skills to manage. And I know the difference between marketing and economic development. So, let me be the first to break it to you, Ava, Tami doesn't have the skills to market heroin to a junky, much less the knowledge to attract development."

The air in the room hung like a black cloud. One of the Town Board members changed the direction of the conversation, "Ya' know, we never have formally defined Mike's job position. Perhaps we need to sit down and do that?" The others agreed, and then proceeded to axe two out of the three conferences from my budget. The conference they didn't put on the chopping block was a land use conference in Denver. Then they set a date for another work session to define my job once and for all. I packed up my lap-top and left, more or less in a huff, in an effort to reaffirm the many ambiguous facets of my being.

On the way home, I could not shake the thought that I had been duped—brought to town on the promise by the Town Board that my job was economic development and land use planning. That they needed someone to make sense of the wolf at the door and even invite it in, so long as it was on a leash. I came to town knowing that it was a blank slate, a white canvas awaiting a paint brush. The enormously fulfilling potential of the job position, from exercising economic development theory to exercising urban design theory, appeared to be lost. If I could not practice the elements of planning that filled my soul with warmth, or any elements of planning for that matter, then what the hell was I doing there? Equally as important, why did the Town Board even hire me?

That night, in early November, only five months after leaving Lawrence and starting my job with La Blanca Gente, I drank a bottle of wine with my wife, and we made a conscious and deliberate decision to actively look for new employment opportunities. I'd had enough.

The next morning, I walked into Town Hall and Ava says in her most chipper voice, "Good morning, Mike, how are you?" She never sounded so chipper. I knew I had lost a battle, but the war was not over. Later that day the mayor stopped by and gave me a list of "priorities" that needed to be dealt with. The biggest was taking an inventory of streets and cataloging what streets were in the most disrepair. What a surprise, Mr. KDOT wants me to deal with freakin' street repair.

I was depressed and un-motivated for a couple of days. I avoided, to the best of my ability, pouting around Town Hall, but I fear I failed. The sad part is for the past couple of weeks I was feeling strong and confident, doing my thing, helping the town, but now I felt horrible, and didn't want to help anybody.

Each night after work I proceeded to cruise the usual planning job postings, mostly through APA's website. Like snow flakes falling across the country, application packets fell into the laps of human resource directors from state to state. With only five months of experience behind me, I knew my odds were long of landing a gig that stroked my ego. Nonetheless, I shot for the top, applying for senior planner positions, which usually require at least three-years of experience, as well as any position that had the word "director" in it. If I could get a director position out of graduate school, then I could get a director position five months later.

I weighed my options.

It became clear to me the gravity of the up-coming meeting: it was a referendum on what the Town Board members really wanted—change or the status quo, Ava calling the shots or giving me free reign to deal with the means while the Town Board discusses the ends. I decided it was time to cash in some favors.

I called the biggest power-broker in town—Grady Ryan—and informed him of the gravity of the situation. He said in his usual cool, calm voice, "Mike, don't worry about a thing, I'll make some calls and we'll show up to that work session to make it clear that the time for screwing around is over." I felt a little better after that conversation; not so much because of Grady's reassurance, but because a plan was slowly forming in my head: get everybody I know, everybody that agrees with my philosophy of doing things, get them to this work session, pitch forks and torches in hand, and the Town Board will have no choice but to see things my way.

I worked behind the scenes, more and more seeing the brilliance in what I was doing. Ava, Tami, the Town Board, are all accustomed to the usual empty work sessions where nobody shows up but town employees and the bosses. If I get the conference room packed with supporters, it will send a clear message of what needs to be done. The best part is Ava would be infuriated.

I lobbied everybody I knew—my neighbors, the local bartender, the clerk at the liquor store, the freakin' postman, it didn't matter, so long as they showed. The campaign grew as the days passed. The meeting was set for the Monday after Thanksgiving. In the meantime, I sent out a flurry of resumes to cover my ass against anything going wrong. I didn't think there was too much of a chance for me to lose my job at this meeting, but, if things didn't swing my way, I would just nod, smile, and say, "you're the bosses, I'll do as you see fit," all the while knowing that a month or two later I'll be accepting a position somewhere else.

Even if the meeting does swing my way, my biggest problems will still persist. Ava, of course, will always be around. Another problem is I've spent my best arguments for economic development methods already. I can say nothing new, nothing creative. At this point I'm just an echo chamber. I came into my position like a hurricane, which, in retrospect, is not the brightest way to go about doing things. A more effective way to get things done is to make the board feel as if they came up with a given idea, empower them to feel as if they are the original ones. The board has shot down time and again my best ideas: create a "Highway Corridor Plan," reduce minimum lot sizes in commercial zones and zeroed-out set-backs, initiate a weekly farmers' market in the summer time, insert some Goddamn urban design guidelines into the land use code, start an urban renewal authority, send me to development conferences. Their rejection of these ideas is not their fault, it's mine. I need to hold their hands, plant the seeds, and watch the ideas germinate in their heads. What it really boils down to is, if I am looking to actually get something done, I need to exercise three fundamental traits that are critical for the success of, not only me, but any planner: patience, modesty, and good politicking.

One must exercise patience because government, pluralism, and consensus building take time. There is a saying among bureaucrats that, "no good idea goes un-punished." The "punishment" for a good idea is consensus building. This is where one must endure a barrage of skepticism and obstructionism. And it takes time to walk through such a process, so be patient.

Modesty is critical. Never take credit for a good idea. Always foist credit onto those who can help you, like the politicians, despite whether or not they have earned it. This will produce for you many allies. For egotistical pricks, such as me, this is perhaps the most difficult factor to implement. Additionally, modesty is critical because one must be calculating and strategic about how to push an initiative forward. Sometimes, perhaps more often than not, this means choosing your battles very carefully, despite the urges you may feel otherwise. That is to say, be modest about what wars are worth waging.

Good politicking is the final piece of the puzzle. Always work the back room. Always work the phones. Strive for casual encounters with those who can help you, like having a beer with a city council person after work. Never suggest something new and bold during public meetings until you are certain the consensus is there to back your play. Likewise, information is power. Use it to your advantage. You would be surprised at how eager city council people and other civic power brokers are to hear the nuances and inner workings of the policy formulation process. Use this information to build your trail of breadcrumbs that lead policy makers to approval of your initiative.

In La Blanca Gente, my biggest problem is not Ava, Tami, or the Town Board. My biggest problem is me. I gave them too much too fast. Worse yet, I was telling them what to do—no modesty. I suggested too many ideas during public meetings—bad politicking. And, I have no patience for consensus building. Because of this, I fear, perhaps the best thing to do is take the lessons learned and ramble-on to the next job. But first, I need to make it through this meeting.

The day of the meeting arrived. Still recovering from a long weekend in the Denver metro, I prepared by writing a list of arguments I could use in the event I need to rebut someone else's. Likewise, if things got really ugly, I prepared a memo to the Town Board that said, "Attached you will find two work samples: one is Tami's 2004 'Marketing Plan,' the other is a Commercial Market Analysis I have recently completed. Please evaluate both products and conclude who you feel is more capable of stimulating economic development."

I arrived early to the meeting and sat anxiously in the Town Hall conference room awaiting the shit-storm. Seven o'clock rolled around and there were no compatriots to be seen. I was worried. If no one shows, I'm screwed. Suddenly, my wife calls; she's out in the parking lot, "Would it be weird if I came in?" She asked. "I see four or five people heading for the door." Feeling a sense of partial relief, I told her to come on in. Seven-ten PM, the meeting starts. Two local business owners, a former Town Board member, his wife, and my wife and daughter are the only supporters I could muster after two weeks of lobbying. Damnit! Where is everybody?

The meeting starts. Everyone's nervous. I hesitate to look anyone in the eyes, including my bosses. Ava's sitting at the end of the conference room table. The mayor chime's up, "Well, Mike, I read the memo you submitted describing how you see your job. Did everyone else read it?" My other bosses sat in silence, reluctant, evidently, to answer his question.

I chimed up: "I'm curious what you guys think of the bulleted list on the second page. Does that sound like a reasonable set of responsibilities?" I plagiarized the list from various planning director job postings on the internet, plugged it into my memo, and claimed it as my own.

The Town Board sat mute as they looked over the list. Only five board members showed up for the meeting. Typical. Worse yet, it was the contingent of old-timers with whom new ideas are treated like a bad case of crabs. Pete, clearly flip-flopping, nodded his head and said, "List looks good to me." A funny statement coming from the man who two weeks earlier said, "Your job is not necessarily for economic development."

His colleagues nodded in agreement. That's when Tyler, a former board member sitting in the audience, decided play-time was over. "Can I say something?" he asked. In my head I could hear the "ding-ding" sound of the bell they use to start and end rounds of boxing. "I think it would be ludicrous for Mike to be working on anything else but economic development. I mean, ya 'know, he's the expert on this stuff and I just want to make sure he's working on it."

I glanced at Ava and caught her rolling her eyes. The mayor responded: "I think you're right, Tyler." I glanced at my lovely wife who was trying to keep herself from laughing. My daughter catches my glance and giggles.

Tyler, in his scruffy Michigan voice, continued: "Ya 'know, why would the Town Board have Mike wasting his time on code enforcement? We all know that code enforcement is the simple part of the equation, ya 'know, I mean, you hardly need a high school diploma to do it."

Give the man a round of applause; he simultaneously helped my cause and slandered Ava.

Feeling better by the minute, I looked to the Town Board for their response, but Tyler wasn't done. "And then you have Tami, who basically is unchecked as the Marketing Director, and I ask you, what has she produced as a result? There are ways to measure the success of a marketing campaign and I suggest you learn what those are and take a hard look at what Tami does over there."

It didn't take long for Tyler to get the crowd fired up. Just then, reinforcements arrived, the two guys I wanted to see most: Grady Ryan and Dalton Roads—the President of the San Luis Valley Economic Development Council and the President of the La Blanca Gente Chamber of Commerce, respectively. Things were getting better by the second. Grady walked up to the conference room table and took a seat alongside the Town Board. What a stud.

Then, a local business owner in the audience decided to chime in: "I took a look at Mike's market analysis; this is quality work that will help the businesses around town plan for the future. Tell me, what has Tami done for the businesses around town to help them, and how do you measure that?"

Wow. The situation was quickly turning into a referendum on Tami, not me. I glanced at Grady and Dalton, they glanced back. Dalton's dad, a man who has sat on the Town Board three times but has yet to win an election, put a stop to the situation. "Before we talk behind an employee's back, we should at least have that employee in the room." His colleagues agreed, but it mattered little.

Grady, from his seat at the big-boys' table, interjected, "Ya 'know, guys, there is a big difference between selling La Blanca Gente and marketing La Blanca Gente. Tami might be good at selling this town, but she is bad at marketing it." The Town Board members stared at each other.

Just then, Truett Tilman walked into the room to join the party. Truett is my age, and I'm coming to find he is more and more of an ally. With his appearance, the Tami reformation ceased and we got down to the business of "what should the Community Development Director be doing?" The Town Board agreed with my interpretation of my job position. I left the meeting feeling up-beat, knowing Ava was pissed and I won the battle that day, which is enough to make any man sing an aria.

Not only did I leave the meeting with a new job description, but I left with a new friend. Tyler stuck his neck out for me during the meeting. From then on, my family and I developed a relationship with Tyler and his family. I thought it only appropriate to have a drink with them whenever I had the opportunity. His wife, Phyllis, could slug down a bottle of white wine like it was a glass of water. I was quite impressed with her abilities. Their kids played with my daughter, and I graciously fed them all the juicy gossip from Town Hall. My wife and I found them to be a welcome interlude between headaches. After all, everybody needs a drinking buddy. Little did we know we made a deal with the devil that night.

10

Campaign Season

The cold, black of Colorado High Country winters are enough to drive a person out of their mind. Once winter settles in, it suffocates unseasoned outsiders, like the cold hand of death around your neck. Zero-degree mountain air is thin and lifeless. With no soul save the occasional snow storm, winter in the Colorado Rockies is void of animation and inspires little. Each day like the other: sunny and windy. Each night like the night before: clear and bitterly cold.

Wine, lots of wine, is the only medication for my soul as I plod through the doldrums of winter. Coming home from day after bad day of work, dark by 4:30, bitterly cold by 5:00, the taste of cabernet on my palate, rolling down my esophagus like a warm elixir, was the only therapy that my body and mind hungered after.

Neighborly friendships helped to cleanse my mind, as well, with homemade "apple pie," as Travis and Maria liked to call it. Consisting mostly of rum and select spices, I would sit in their dining room and pine away a Friday night. All the while passing around the apple pie to be swilled from a ceramic jug that we all shared, like cowboys passing around a bottle of whiskey on the open range.

Cabernet, bitterly cold, dark, cigarette smoke, apple pie, municipal politics beating me down. Winter in La Blanca Gente.

"Have some more apple pie, sweetie," Maria would say. "This will warm your soul."

"And put some hair on that scrawny back of yours, Tedesco," Maria's husband, Travis, would say.

Travis and Maria Cavanaugh. One a tried and true Colorado cowboy, the other a tried and true big-city girl. I suspect that Travis won the argument about where to live after they got married.

And as Travis and I would light our respective cigarettes, Maria always kept a cold, American beer in our hands. "Thanks, baby. I sure do love you," Travis would say.

"I'm lucky you do," Maria would respond.

"How's work going, honey, you look tired?"

"I'm a basket case, guys. I don't think I can handle the atmosphere at Town Hall any longer. I'm on my last leg."

"Why do you put up with it, Tedesco?" Travis chimed in. "I would never put up with that shit."

And I believed him, too, because there's something about Colorado cowboys that's principled and true. They all have a line and, if you cross it, they're not afraid to let you know in no uncertain terms. Like tripping a land-mine, Colorado cowboys are just fine until someone steps on them.

My vision clouded by cigarette smoke and my mind clouded by apple pie, Travis and Maria didn't need to prod me much to open up. "So, what do you do about Tami and Ava? I think it's safe to say they're trying to fuck you over," Travis said.

"I think you're right, man. They're pretty shameless about it, too. But one can't be taught how to refute those that formulate opinions predicated on a foundation of ignorance; opinions that materialize in minds that operate in the absence of logic and reason. How does one respond to such silliness?"

"Swill of apple pie, big guy?"

"Travis, you are indeed wise," I said as I took the bottle from his outstretched hands.

"You seem down, man. Is there anything we can do to help?" Travis asked.

"I don't know." I paused and thought for a moment as I drew from my cigarette. "Do one of you guys feel like running for the Town Board?" Travis and Maria just laughed.

With a smile, I shake my head to their response and continued: "I'm assailed by a constant barrage of pre-conceived notions and embarrassing professionalism, my motivation, open-mindedness, and confidence have been chiseled away by an abusive culture that knows little of the world around them and even less about how to operate as respectful and trusting human beings."

"I believe it, I have dealt with both of them before and I'm afraid they are far from charming," Maria said.

"It's an absurd injustice to all those that even pretend to operate with the simplest degree of intelligence. The La Blanca Gente culture, driven by Ava, Tami, and those that agree with them, toy with my sanity, my faith in doing the 'right thing' because it is the right thing to do. In La Blanca Gente, there is no 'right,' only wrong. Those who strive to do the town right will be chastised amongst the local gossipers and criticized in back rooms by those who lack the sack to pony-up to the table and offer a solution. Ava and Tami are winning the war, which is why I have been applying for jobs for the past couple of months. Their spoil is the fact that I'll leave town with my head down, defeated."

"I don't know if I would characterize it as defeat, Tedesco," Travis chimed in. "You're doing what you need to do given the situation at hand. I don't disrespect you for that."

As I exhale cigarette smoke, I shake my head in frustration then take a gulp of some beer. "I pity the poor fool that follows, for my story will be catalogued into the annals of La Blanca Gente history and passed along from generation to generation as an example on how not to do things. The magical irony being Ava and Tami, as they pine away fruitless and uninspired careers as La Blanca Gente administrators, will point at the example I set and cite it when telling new employees about the wrong way to operate as a professional. When, all the while, they should be pointing at themselves. My head should be stuffed and mounted on the wall above Ava's desk as a reminder to those that follow that all attempts to tamper with the town's deeply rooted malaise will only result in mockery. Ava is the gatekeeper. Tami, too foolish to understand, is only Ava's pet goat. Tami operates in the absence of intelligence. Ava, however, is a maniacal and conniving La Blanca Gente fundamentalist. Ava's smart enough to know that if change comes to La Blanca Gente, all that she knows in this universe will change with it and, in all likelihood, she will not be able to wield the influence that she now levies. Without question, Ava will never be turned away from a philosophy of distrust and prejudice. The most intelligent, thoughtful opinion the Town of La Blanca Gente Board of Trustees could render in an effort to make La Blanca Gente a better place is to fire Ava and thereby rid Town Hall of one who instigates a fundamentally flawed, closed-minded, and negative viewpoint of life in general. Because La Blanca Gente Town Hall and all that comes with it is the only life Ava knows, she has no choice but to exercise her putrid venom within those walls, poisoning all those who enter, corrupting the minds of unsuspecting elected officials who, like I, only entered by the motivation to 'do the right thing,' whatever that definition might entail. A suffocating ignorance. Slowly and painfully, it is Ava's opinion that wraps around you like a python, choking off any and all notions of change, notions driven by the dictates of reality, notions that drive elected officials to run for the Town Board and brave the unending scrutiny that comes with it. So long as Ava pulls the strings in La Blanca Gente Town Hall, the community will never become a better place, will never evolve into a true 'community.' There is no hope."

"Wow, Tedesco. You must stay up nights thinking about this stuff. You're a basket case, man," Travis said.

"One must be a baboon to compete with the baboons. Not a thousand poets with a thousand years to write could accurately articulate the frustration I feel."

"Well said, Tedesco, well said indeed."

"I would do well if one of you two ran for the Town Board."

Travis looked at Maria. Maria at me: "More apple pie, sweetie?"

In late fall, a new music store opened in La Blanca Gente. Run by a 30-something young man from Illinois, the consensus around town was that the store would fail. After all, how many musicians are in the La Blanca Gente market, anyway?

Now mid-winter, Jackie (the store owner), one way or another, recruited a prominent country western musician to come to La Blanca Gente to play a gig. As it happens, but not surprisingly, this was perhaps the biggest social event in La Blanca Gente's history. It was a hit, attracting over 300 people to the show. Considering the winter population of La Blanca Gente hovers around 1,000, the significance of the occasion cannot be overstated.

Due to the success of this event, Jackie started the La Blanca Gente Music Association (GMA). The first thing on GMA's agenda was to build an outdoor stage to help attract talent and to, eventually, start a La Blanca Gente music festival. With the wind at his back, Jackie presented his idea to the Town Board, which received a positive reception. In the meantime, I was doing everything I could to help Jackie with the project. We knew we had to capture the momentum before the La Blanca Gente rumor mill put a stop to it. The band-shell itself would have cost the town no money to erect, only the land to put it on.

Jackie's initial proposal to the Town Board to build a band-shell on town property was crisp and to the point. I had supplied him with a dirty laundry list of arguments that the Town Board will likely toss back to him. In his presentation, he put a stop to all such arguments. And, in the end, the Town Board told him to put together a plan, i.e., estimations of capacity for each potential site in town and come back next month to present it to them. "No problem," was Jackie's response.

Late one cold, January, Friday afternoon, the mayor and his wife came into Town Hall to ask Ava a couple of questions on various topics. The subject of the conversation shifted to the GMA band-shell. Like a vulture circling a kill, Ava took the opportunity to swoop in. "I think it would be best if this went on private property rather than town property— the town has no business getting into the music business," Ava said.

"You think so?" the mayor said.

"Yes I do," Ava responded. "This thing is going to cause a lot of problems with crime, and drinking, and the like. What if there is a fight during an event? How are we going to manage parking for events? How do we know that Jackie even knows what he is doing? This thing will either be too much for the town to handle or a total failure."

The mayor, in response, just said, "Well, we'll see what happens at the meeting."

As Ava spoke, I started to gather my things. Not in the mood to bicker with Ava regarding her fallacy laden arguments, I bit my lip and prepared to follow the mayor home for a chat. The mayor and his wife left Town Hall. I packed up and followed him home. "Hey Mike, what are you doing here?" he asked as I walked up to him in his driveway.

"Do you have a couple minutes to talk?" I replied.

"Sure, come on in." he said as he closed the door to his truck.

We went inside. His house is small, yet a good size for two people. As I declined a soda from Pete's wife, I sat down to talk. I went straight into business: "I gotta tell ya, Pete, Ava really upsets me when she spreads her skepticism and negativity to you like she just did a couple of minutes ago.

It's not her job to give opinions on projects like this nor is she qualified to do so."

"I agree," the mayor said.

"That's good to hear," I said quickly, not quite done venting to him. "Ya' know, Pete, she says this stuff and she doesn't back it up with facts. Her arguments are driven more by paranoia than logic."

Pete replied, "I know, it irritates me, too."

After his statement, Pete officially took the floor. Evidently, after Pete's first term in office, when he was up for re-election, Ava was campaigning against him. Naturally, this T'd Pete off. Likewise, at least this is what he told me, Pete is well aware of the problems with Ava and there is growing talk around La Blanca Gente to get her the hell out of Town Hall. According to Pete, he only makes Ava feel like she's in the middle of everything just to keep her "off my back." This was a fairly compelling argument, and I bought it, to a certain degree.

Pete takes his counsel from the local "coffee circle"—a group of old-timers that gather every morning in the local coffee shop to gossip about the goings-on in the Valley. Pete excluded, these are the old men who have weathered many a lean La Blanca Gente winter and managed to survive it all. These are the old men who campaigned against La Blanca Gente incorporating in 1993 and still cite the event as one of the worst happenings in La Blanca Gente's history. These are the old men who see no need to trifle with land use codes and good planning. These are the old men that drive common opinion in La Blanca Gente.

Pete continued giving me inside information, including, but not shockingly, that Elroy Potus is the only one on the Town Board that thought I was doing a poor job. Elroy has little credibility amongst his fellow board members, however, because of his sexual liaisons with the Town Clerk. Additionally, chances are the guy can drink a Jesuit sommelier under the table. To judge him a lush is somewhat of an understatement.

"So what can we do, Pete?"

"You gotta learn the game, Mike. Learn the game."

Pete's choice of words demonstrated a degree of wisdom behind his statement. I couldn't change the game; all I could do was play it to the best of my abilities. It's a chess match, and both teams utilize their respective pawns to out flank the other: me with the business elite, and Ava and Tami with Elroy utilizing their credibility with the locals to spread their gospel to anyone who will listen.

It was time for me to start planting the seeds of reform throughout town—to play the game. With an April 6th municipal election only a couple of months away, and five seats on the Town Board up for grabs, it was time for me to transition from compliant Community Development Director to closet campaign manager. To stack the Town Board with five, pro-Tedesco trustees would represent a majority and therefore a quantum shift in the political dialectic.

I quickly learned that campaign season is a maddening time for professional bureaucrats, particularly if the slate is packed with those who wish to change the current status quo. For those who have grown numb, for those who have lost motivation, for those bureaucrats who only work the position because it's a job and they get paid for it, campaign season exposes their soft underbelly. As it is in the business world it is in government: a change in management might spell layoffs. Doing my part to stack the ballot with pro-Tedesco candidates was one of my few pleasures as winter grew long.

By February 14th, Valentines Day, upwards of two months before the April 6th municipal election, I had convinced three political newcomers to run for the Town Board. The Anti-Ava, Give Mike Tedesco a Raise Campaign was in full swing. There were two other possible newcomers I would prefer to see not get elected. Thus, with five seats on the line, seven newcomers would place their names on the ballot. Three of the five incumbents would again place their names on the ballot. Five seats for ten candidates, a high-risk high-reward situation.

Of the three incumbents re-running, one of them was Elroy, Ava's boyfriend. I already knew, as did the whole town, that he drove his El Camino into the Rio Grande River one night and he's now on probation for driving while intoxicated as a result. If this was enough to kill his re-election campaign remained to be seen.

It was Elroy who routinely chimed up during board meetings to challenge me on my assertions. It was Elroy who Ava gossiped with over the phone just about every morning planting seeds of hate and doubt into his mind. It was Elroy who decided to run for re-election because, as he said it to me, "I think this town has some folks making decisions that just don't understand what they are doing, and I need to be around to challenge them on that."

In order to beat Elroy, I needed to come at him sideways. He, being one-seventh my boss, meant that a full frontal attack was out of the question. The only thing I can do to counter Elroy's libido-driven, pro-Ava viewpoint was to run a closet campaign against him. And, better yet, convince close friends to run on a pro-Tedesco ticket.

At the top of my list was Phyllis Baine. Her husband, Tyler, went to bat for me at the meeting where the Town Board had a public referendum on my job description. It was Tyler who had already served time on the Town Board and knows the games that Ava and Tami play all too well. And, after a month or so of prodding, I had convinced Phyllis of the virtues of running for the Town Board.

Phyllis was my silver bullet, the one soul in La Blanca Gente I can count on to speak-up during uncomfortable moments and state the truth. I had told Phyllis everything. I armed her with all the ammo she needed to succeed as a trustee, and she appeared poised to do so. If anybody can change the discourse at Town Hall, it would be Phyllis, and I'm pleased that she is running.

It only took three or four Fridays of passing around the apple pie for me to convince Maria Cavanaugh to run for the Town Board. No doubt, having a compatriot like Maria on the Town Board would provide big returns.

Looking at Pete, sitting in his living room, and listening to him chatter on, I knew that if only a couple of pro-Tedesco candidates won seats on the board, Ava and Tami would awake to a new day.

Pete finished up his conversation with me by saying, "Ya' know, Mike, I'm running uncontested for mayor, so chances are I'll be around a while. If you have a beef, don't be afraid to come talk with me."

"You bet, Pete," I said as I shook his hand. I left the mayor's house feeling alright about the conversation and drove down to the local liquor store for a bottle of La Blanca Gente's finest. Next door to the liquor store was an arts and craft store and the business owner was outside tinkering with this and that. "Jack, what are you doing, man?" I half yelled from the adjacent parking lot.

"Hey Mike, come over here, I want to talk with you about a thing or two."

I was hoping he would say that, because he was half convinced to run for the Town Board. Jack's an active civic participant in the La Blanca Gente area, and he's built like an offensive lineman. "What do you think I should do?" he asked me. "I'm gonna run, this town is fucked-up. I think it's worth the time," Jack said, answering his own question.

"I think that's a good decision, man," I responded.

"Let me buy you a drink, Mike. You can fill me in on all the dirty details."

"You got yourself a deal, I'll meet you at the bar." And thus the pro-Tedesco ticket placed a third candidate. I'd lobbied three people since Christmas to run for the Town Board and Jack, God bless his heart, finally conceded to my counsel.

11

The Village at Wolf Creek

Located just up the road from La Blanca Gente is the continental divide and Wolf Creek ski area. Wolf Creek routinely receives more snow than any other ski hill in the State of Colorado. Not a bad distinction considering the competition. The ski slope is family owned and small, in relative terms, compared to its competition. The reclusive Teeter family owns and operates the hill. It was only recently when they decided to join the Colorado Ski Association—a hallmark of all Colorado ski destinations. Their market range is mostly regional, serving the San Luis Valley and the other side of the continental divide (e.g., Pagosa Springs, Durango, and vicinity). Only by accident and circumstance does the slope attract interstate and international visitors. One may be able to argue, as some do, that because of the Teeter family's reluctance to market their hill, resort town growth has been stunted in La Blanca Gente.

The Teeter family may want to keep their hill a small, regional operation; but the owner of a pro football team and, not to mention, the largest car dealer in one of the largest states in the country (where everything is big), has other ideas. Buckley Hasslbeck intends to turn roughly 300 acres at the base of the Teeter's hill into a premier Colorado ski village, that is to say, a "world class" destination, attracting only those with deep enough pockets to play, and employing only those with shallow enough pockets to work.

Nonetheless, if one puts on their developer's hat, it's not hard to see the attraction (profit potential) of the site. Thus the saga begins: The Village at Wolf Creek, or "the Village" as locals call it. A classic case of development versus the environment, economics versus preservation, capitalism versus the San Luis Valley, a powder keg, a tinder box, a reason for the uninformed to read the paper, mass hysteria.

The President of the local Chamber of Commerce, an ally of mine, has buddied up with the front man—Billy Jacto—on the Village project. Likewise, the town attorney's wife, also an attorney, and one whom I consider a friend, is working as legal counsel for an environmental group lobbying to stop the project. Thus, with one hand, I'm shaking hands and flashing a warm smile to the President of the Chamber of Commerce, and with the other hand I'm passing a bottle of wine to the town attorney's wife as she and her husband routinely join me and my wife for dinner.

Billy Jacto is a Texas local with a shady history and an even shadier way of doing business. My first week on the job, I was invited to a morning meeting where Billy was the keynote speaker. He shook my hand and made me feel warm and fuzzy with his Southern charm, but it doesn't take a genius to figure out the man is a snake-oil salesman. A former city manager for a large town on the horizontal yellow of Texas, rumor has it he got fired for embezzlement. Nothing major, or so I hear, no jail time, but embezzlement is embezzlement. It also doesn't help that he treats locals with the attitude that we're hillbillies, which is mostly an accurate depiction, but it certainly doesn't help.

We talked for a few moments, Billy and I, discussed possibly working out some kind of deal on housing. He gave me his card, and that was that. It was all bullshit because I never heard from him. Until, one day, a couple months later, I was fishing for some accurate Village build-out projections to utilize in my Market Analysis. I pulled out Billy's card and called him at his Austin, Texas office. I felt a bit strange calling the front man on a billion dollar project to ask a favor, but what the hell.

"Billy, how ya doing. This is Mike Tedesco with the Town of La Blanca Gente."

"Who?" Billy replied.

"Mike Tedesco. I'm the Community Development Director for the Town of La Blanca Gente."

"What do you want?" he asked.

"I'm putting together a market analysis for the Town of La Blanca Gente and I'm curious if you could email me the build-out projections for the Village?"

"Why would I do that?" Billy said with a tone.

"To do me and the Town of La Blanca Gente a favor; it's nothing special, just email me all the numbers that are already part of the public record so I could put together this analysis with accurate projections."

"Tell ya what," Billy said. "Email me exactly what you need and I'll see if I can't get you the numbers."

Click. He hung up the phone without even saying good-bye. I emailed him my request. Naturally, he never responded, and I didn't expect him to. Needless to say, the day he comes strutting into my office, with that cocky Texas attitude, asking me to help on one thing or another, I'll make sure and return the favor.

It was roughly six months before I saw him again. We ended up at the same meeting and, true to form, he introduced himself to me like he had no idea who I was. For my part, true to form, I pretended like I didn't hear his, "Hi, Billy Jacto, nice to meet ya." I turned my back to him and walked away. My grudge, however, had yet to play itself out.

After the meeting I had an interesting conversation with one of the Valley power brokers. He told me what I already knew; that Billy is all talk and makes a living irritating the locals. We concurred that Buckley would be better served hiring a different front man for the Village project.

Rumor has it that Billy's right hand man, the President of the La Blanca Gente Chamber of Commerce and a vocal ally of mine as well as the Village project, is in Billy's back pocket. I don't know if he gets paid regularly or what, but the word on the street is he is financially vested in the project. I like to gossip just as much as the next girl, but normally I do not give much credence to what is cranked out of the Valley rumor mill. On this instance, however, the source of such conjecture is the attorney for the environmental activist group trying to stop the Village project.

Holly Messina, Tony's wife, works as pro bono legal counsel trying to put a stop to the project. She also works part time for the Teeter family on their ski hill, updating snow reports and selling lift tickets. Rumor has it, and this rumor comes from Dalton—Billy's right hand man in La Blanca Gente and President of the local Chamber of Commerce—that Holly gets paid much more than the typical ticket booth operator at Wolf Creek ski area. Thus, both sides are blaming each other for being in somebody's back pocket.

Even though residents of the San Luis Valley are divided by the Village project, on the other side of the pass there's little ambiguity when it comes to their opinion. Pagosa Springs is obstinately against it; so much so that the Pagosa Springs Town Board, in a symbolic statement, voted to denounce the project. In a symbolic response, the La Blanca Gente Town Board voted to support the project. When one steps back and looks at the larger picture, these dueling banjos, even though their efforts are largely meaningless, reflect the chasm in attitude and philosophy separated by a short drive and the continental divide.

Joel Garreau wrote about this in his book, *The Nine Nations of North America*. He dubbed the Pacific coast from San Francisco up through about Juneau, Alaska, "Ecotopia."[39] The name is self-explanatory. East of Ecotopia, over the crest of the Cascade ranges and into the rain shadows, he dubbed "The Empty Quarter."[40] The name is self-explanatory, if not a bit dated. The Empty Quarter spanned the breadth of the intermountain West, including the Canadian Rockies. Although Garreau's book came out in 1981, his geographic distinctions are still accurate. Twenty-eight years later, however, The Empty Quarter is less empty. This because residents of Ecotopia (and residents of New England and the East Coast) have "discovered" the intermountain West and, by doing so, have brought their espresso machines, micro breweries, mountain bikes, hiking boots, skis, snowboards, and preservation ideologies with them. Thus, and anyone who has even a passing interest in demographics and geography knows this intuitively, ever expanding pockets of Ecotopia are now within and influencing the future of The Empty Quarter.

The quarrel over the Village at Wolf Creek is a classic case of Ecotopia versus The Empty Quarter. Or, perhaps more precisely, the Old West versus the New West. La Blanca Gente and the San Luis Valley being the Old West, hungry for growth and development (yet scared and threatened by change in general), Pagosa Springs being the New West (people whom embrace change yet are inclined to preserve).

The physical geography of the matter makes the difference all the more prescient. La Blanca Gente, stuck in the rain shadow of Wolf Creek Pass and the San Juan Mountains, brown, sagebrush, Pinon pines; and Pagosa Springs, on the Wolf Creek up-slope, lush, green, inviting; and the proposed Village at Wolf Creek stuck right in the middle of it all. From all vantage points—economic, cultural, and physical—there's no surprise: the Village is the camel that brings all these issues to the forefront.

We know by now, as Gundars Rudzitis knows, that "The future of the West, particularly in high amenity places, is of dependence on another type of export industry, tourism and recreation, a playground oriented development strategy."[41] Buckley Hasslbeck, Wolf Creek ski area, and even the Town of La Blanca Gente, fit well into such a notion.

The history of the West is strewn with tales of development versus the environment. In the past, however, "development" was the procession of logging, ranching, and mining initiatives into virgin wilderness. Ghosts of the Old West still haunt the New West but the discourse has evolved, as embodied by the proposed Village at Wolf Creek, into preserving virgin lands from becoming Meccas for the rich to play and the surrounding environs to become exploited. Simply, the locals do not want Wolf Creek to turn into another Aspen. As Timothy Egan says in *Lasso the Wind*, "If land and religion are what people most often kill each other over, then the West is different only in that the land is the religion."[42]

From my vantage point, I feel conflicted about the entire project. On one hand, if I was an outsider learning about the Village project with no other knowledge of the region, I would rally behind the Ecotopian's banner of preservation. On the other hand, as one who is just starting my career, the Village will no doubt provide the all important tipping point for La Blanca Gente to tap the Ecotopian, New West market; as such, on my resume, I could claim, true or not, to be the one who brought La Blanca Gente from rags to riches. Not to mention, I need to tow my bosses' line of supporting the project.

The day of reckoning cometh, however. On April 7th, 2006, supporters and critics of the Village met for a showdown. Organized by the San Luis Valley Economic Development Council (EDC), a debate was arranged in an attempt to "put all the facts on the table" and to try and set the record straight. Grady Ryan—Stud Incarnate—was to facilitate the discussion. Grady, who is President of the San Luis Valley EDC and a vocal proponent for the Village, was to moderate the debate. Grady is a man of high character and even higher charisma; however, I question his decision to moderate in lieu of soliciting a neutral moderator.

On behalf of the San Luis Valley EDC, Grady invited a slue of state and national legislators, as well as the primary opponent of the Village: Colorado Wild. Like a ballistics magician, Grady put together the ingredients for an explosion. The showdown was to take place in the Town of Creede. (Creede being the County Seat of the county that encompasses Wolf Creek.) Holly told me that since the EDC was going to facilitate the meeting, she didn't feel comfortable with the situation.

She went on to tell me that perhaps Colorado Wild would stage some type of "rally" before the event.

It's tough having professional acquaintances and friends on both sides of this issue, because a part of me felt like I should tell (warn) Grady and Dalton of the impending "rally." But, by doing so, I would betray Holly's trust. Thus is City Planners' rub.

The day of the big meeting was rapidly approaching. Four days prior, on Monday, April 3rd, our trusty friends at the U.S. Forest Service released the final draft of the Village at Wolf Creek Environmental Impact Statement (EIS). In short, they approved what was necessary for the development to move forward. It just so happens that on that same day Jackie, who is the president of the La Blanca Gente Music Association, and I had a meeting with a Bureau of Land Management (BLM) representative to collect some info on putting a band-shell on BLM land. Jackie and I traveled to the BLM office, which doubles as a Forest Service office. We met with a BLM bureaucrat and got squared away. On our way out the door, low and behold, in came Grady and Dalton. "I wonder what you guys are doing here?" I said with sarcasm. Grady smiled his usual mustache framed smile. Dalton nodded his head. Jackie and I decided to stick around and chat with the boys after their business was done. They picked up the EIS and, as we were heading out the door, low and behold, in walks Albert Williams, staff employee of one honorable U.S. Representative Mike S. Armijo, the arch enemy of the Village project.

Now, it just so happens that Jackie and the La Blanca Gente Music Association were due to have a sit down with Mr. Williams to try and lobby his boss to insert a line item into any given House Bill that would give away that slice of BLM heaven to the Town of La Blanca Gente. Unfortunately, prior to that day, we had never met him. Grady, Dalton, and Albert exchange hellos. "So did your boss receive the invitation to the forum on Friday?" Grady asked, innocently enough. "Ya, we got it, but we're not sure if his schedule is clear for that night," Albert replied, politically enough. "Alright, well," Grady continued, "we'd love to have him if he can make it." At that, the conversation closed. Jackie and I looked at each other both thinking the same thing: "Holy shit! That's Albert Williams." We walked out with Albert and introduced ourselves. Outside, within ear shot of Grady and Dalton, Albert asked, "Are you with them?"

"Yes," I replied, now very worried. "They're helping us with the band-shell project." Albert glanced over at the two. "Oh," he responded. "Well, it was nice to meet you guys."

Damn. That was a heavy situation. Running into Albert, Grady, and Dalton at the Forest Service office on the day that the EIS for the Village went public and at the same time trying to grease Albert's wheels on the band-shell. "You guys want to do lunch?" I hollered to Grady and Dalton. "Sure thing. Let's head into Monte Vista." Albert got in his car and left.

During the ride to Monte Vista, Jackie and I were quick to decide that it would be best to call Albert and make sure it was clear that we were not "with Grady and Dalton" in the political sense, and that the whole thing was just a coincidence. Also during the car ride, Jackie and I realized the gravity of the moment—eating lunch with the two most vocal proponents of the Village on the day the Federal government gave it the green light to proceed.

Inside Nino's Restaurant in downtown Monte Vista, Grady and Dalton pretty much owned the place. People came up to shake their hands. Grady was hollering across the crowded dining room to say "hello" and crack a smart-ass remark to people I didn't recognize. Every other person that walked through the door knew either Grady or Dalton. In the meantime, Jackie and I just sat there trying to keep our composure.

It was Grady and Dalton's moment of glory. They knew it, too. With what amounted to Federal approval of the Village project, there appeared to be no more regulatory hurdles for the development to jump over. All Jackie and I could do was sit back and chuckle about the monumental nature of the moment. We all ate burritos and speculated on when the Village might start construction.

As we all pined away the next four days, our anxiety grew. Word of the big showdown caught the attention of Colorado Public Radio, as well as the local newspapers in Denver and Pueblo. As word spread across the state of the upcoming showdown, murmurs grew that the event was a staged concoction with the San Luis Valley Economic Development Council stirring the cocktail. In a symbolic act of defiance, Colorado State Representative Mark Larson (R-Cortez) and State Senator Jim Isgar (D-Durango) published an official Colorado State House of Representatives press release, stating, among other things, "Faced with an agenda stacked to prevent a free exchange of ideas, Colorado Legislators concerned about the impacts of the proposed Village at Wolf Creek are boycotting the proposed April 7th forum in Creede . . ."[43]

In what seemed like an effort to add to the tension, the Mineral County Sheriff's Office called-in additional law enforcement as back-up from Pueblo County. The massive influence of law enforcement led one reporter to opine, "For a time Friday evening there were more law enforcement officers walking this rustic mining town's main street than there were residents."[44]

Unfazed by all the negative publicity, Stud Incarnate and the San Luis Valley EDC pressed onward. The San Luis Valley EDC's Board of Directors consists of a prominent city manager for a relatively large town in the Valley, not to mention the San Luis County administrator. Insisting that the decisions being made to facilitate the forum were unbiased, the San Luis Valley EDC's Board of Directors dismissed the lack of participation as partisan politics.

Friday, April 7th, 2006. A day that anxiety hung in the air throughout the San Luis Valley and perhaps even on the Pagosa Springs' side of the mountains as well. The meeting was scheduled for 6:00 that evening. No doubt lured by the promise of a good show, my wife and daughter decided to tag along with me to the event.

We left at 5:30 that evening to drive up the road to Creede. We arrived to the forum venue about 10 minutes early—an old vacated mine that has been converted into a museum. Outside, locals and law enforcement officials walked restlessly throughout the premises. I stepped out of the car and glanced around to survey the situation. No visible protesters—probably for the best.

As we made our way inside, we were handed a flyer entitled, "Why all the controversy?" which attempted to derail any notion of San Luis Valley EDC credibility. I gave a nod to the La Blanca Gente Chief of Police, who was in his civilian attire but chatting with a group of law enforcement officials. My family and I stepped into the crowded meeting room.

Most of the seats were already taken. On the seats still unclaimed, there sat an agenda as well as a four page document titled, "History – Village at Wolf Creek." The San Luis Valley EDC produced the document as a hand-out to the audience. Cherry-picking quotes from various rulings and approval documents that have been recorded since the saga began in 1986, the "History" document clearly was biased in favor of the project. Nowhere within the stack of papers sitting upon each person's seat was there documentation illustrating a dissenting viewpoint.

My family and I sat next to Pete and his wife right in the front row. Stud Incarnate came over to shake our hands; I wished him luck and told him to "stay out of trouble" as he walked off to prepare for the start of the meeting. The podium was flanked by two long tables. At one table was Buckley Hasslbeck and his henchman—Billy Jacto. At the other were a couple of random folks I did not recognize. Sitting detached from the audience in their own little cluster were the other six board members for the San Luis Valley EDC.

My wife and I looked nervously around the crowded venue, while my daughter sat innocently swinging her legs back and forth beneath her chair.

Grady, after shaking hands with a couple of reporters, approached the podium to start the meeting. By now, the room was so full, crowds of people stood where they could find room because all the seats were taken.

As Grady introduced himself and his colleagues on the San Luis Valley EDC Board of Directors, a group of protesters inched their way in through the crowded front door, silently holding signs voicing their dissent for all to see. Grady ignored them as if they were not present and began reading the "Rules of Conduct" for the forum. One of the rules was complete and total subservience to the moderator. Apparently, the Mineral County Sheriff's office granted Grady carte blanche authority over the forum. Grady always did have a way of talking people into doing things.

Because no opposing viewpoints accepted the San Luis Valley EDC's invitation to participate, only people who supported the project were seated on stage. Grady granted Buckley Hasslbeck a five minute opening statement. Trying to paint himself as an innocent victim, Buckley played to the crowd best he could. During Buckley's statements, his Henchman produced large, glossy, poster-board renderings of the project and placed them on easels for all to see.

Then it was Jamie Welsh's turn—the Mineral County Land Use Administrator, my counterpart. Jamie spent his five minutes describing the almost 20-year approval process that Buckley and his team had gone through just to get to this point. Jamie, almost bragging, said he'd been around for every step of it.

As Grady transitioned the forum into the open questions segment, he was interrupted by a protestor who'd finally had enough of the charade. Heckling from the back of the room, "Why don't you give dissenting viewpoints a chance to speak? This whole meeting is a farce!"

Grady, with a look that suggested "what took you so long," asked the heckler to please sit down and said, "if you have any questions, please write them down and we'll address them one at a time." But the heckler did not get a chance to respond. Law enforcement officials swooped in to escort him away. Some crowd members booed at the sight of this. Others cheered. Many, like me, just sat and enjoyed the show.

Thus was the only theatre of the entire event, however. The rest of the evening was spent allowing Buckley and his henchman to carry the discussion. Caitlin and I left quite disappointed. All the local and regional papers ran their articles the next day trying to sensationalize the event. But for those of us who attended we knew it was all bluster. The San Luis Valley EDC's attempt to provide a neutral forum clearly failed. They did, however, manage to sell their credibility to shine a spotlight on the controversy.

12

On the Hunt

S pring in the Colorado High Country is slow and deliberate. It's nothing like the warm/cold roller coaster rides much of the rest of the country experiences. No, in the Rockies, spring happens a degree at a time, over days at a time, and it takes weeks to notice the difference. There are no dramatic warm fronts ushering in humid, southerly winds; just cold, thin air trying its best to respond to the ever heightening sun.

I'm waiting to hear back regarding a job interview I recently had for the Town of Silverthorne, Colorado. Located in Summit County, only miles from Aspen, Vail, and Breckenridge; Silverthorne thrives as a "B" class resort and retail destination. I interviewed for the position of Economic Development Director, and I thought it went well. It's been a week since the interview, however, and with each passing day, my hope dims that I'll be offered the job.

Being a professional searching for a new job, willing to live just about anywhere, there's no such thing as sacrifice to make a job offer happen. Being hopelessly desperate drives a person to say just about anything. I have found through much trial and error that the key to successfully interviewing in the public sector is to hammer home a series of very important points. All of which being factual; what may be disputed, however, is whether or not the interviewee actually believes the B.S. he's singing. One only needs a spotless enough resume to merit a phone call requesting an interview.

The best argument to demonstrate that an aspiring bureaucrat is prepared and mentally qualified to work for any given governmental entity is the notion that, "It's not my job to make policy decisions. That's up to city council. It's my job to effectively administrate potential or adopted policy decisions." Planners, in theory anyway, do not have the luxury of basing their decisions on their own personal values. That's the job of the policy makers, for the policy makers have the luxury of making decisions based on opinions and speculation. Planners can only make decisions based on facts and the opinions that stem from a foundation of them. The planner's hammer, which is a good one by virtue of its effectiveness, is the power to recommend approval or denial of a given policy decision. Nothing will scare the socks off a developer more than saying, "I'm happy to kick this up to city council, but based on the facts at hand, I just can't recommend approval unless you agree to X, Y, and Z."

There is indeed a fine line between "administrative" and "policy" decisions, however. If a planner is an effective communicator, he/she can manipulate their way into wielding both. Of course, that's best left out of the conversation—particularly with people who are considering the merits of hiring you.

If one is interviewing for a lower level planning position, the only item that needs to be said during an interview, like a politician trying to hammer home his talking points, is, "My responsibility is to effectively administrate the policies as set forth internally by my supervisor and more broadly by city council. All I want to do is help my supervisor succeed." If one finds a way to magically tie each answer to each question back to that one singular point then, congratulations, you just got hired.

The same philosophy holds true for upper management in government bureaucracies. But one must twist it a bit differently, such as: "It's my job to administrate decisions that you, as my bosses make. Sometimes, there is a fine line between 'administrative' decisions and 'policy' decisions. If there is even a nagging thought in the back of my head saying, 'maybe I should kick this up to city council,' then you can bet I'm going to kick it up to city council."

Naturally, nine times out of ten, if you're not sure about something, it is a bad idea to kick it up to city council because chances are it will make you look bad as a result. Councils and boards are very bad at making decisions, particularly decisions that you want them to make, because, either out of ego, ignorance, or just show-boating, they'll find a reason to say "no." Simply, avoid, almost at all costs, allowing your council to go on a fishing exhibition for a reason to deny the initiative. If you want them to say "yes" on an initiative, then, as the administrator, you must craftily put them in a box that forces nothing other than a "yes" answer. Do not give them any reason to say "no." More importantly, you must position the initiative in a way that if they do say "no," they look extremely bad doing it, i.e., a "no" answer gives the public yet another reason not to re-elect them. Such is the power that a government administrator holds—the power of perception. We are the gatekeepers.

A month to go before La Blanca Gente election day— Armageddon—I finally get the call from the Silverthorne Town Manager. "Mike, we've made a decision to go a different direction with the Economic Development Director position." Clearly, my philosophy on interviewing needs some adjustment.

"Can I ask what direction you're going?" I replied quite pointlessly and with disappointment.

"We're going to re-post the position and look internally for a candidate."

"I understand. Well, thank you for the opportunity."

Rejection stings. Worse yet, I didn't even get beat-out by a better candidate. Not only did he just tell me that he doesn't want to hire me, he told me not even to bother reapplying for the position. It has been roughly five months and several job applications since that fateful evening in November when I consciously made the decision to leave La Blanca Gente, and still no luck.

A few weeks earlier, I submitted an application packet to the City of Pueblo, Colorado, for a position that appeared to have some promise—Executive Director for their local urban renewal authority. The Baines pointed me to an article in the Pueblo Chieftain regarding how the city was having a hard time filling the position. I knew little about the city other than it's an old, busted steel town and the county line between Pueblo and El Paso County is known by locals as the Tortilla Curtain, because there is a big difference between the upstanding Protestant Whites in Colorado Springs, and the blue-collar Catholic ethnicities in Pueblo.

A week or so later I got the call I was hoping for from Pueblo's Human Resources Department to schedule an interview. Dressed for success in my black, JC Penney's suit, which happened to be the only suit I owned, I walked into Pueblo City Hall for the interview. Greeted by the City Manager, the City's Planning Director, the Chairman of Pueblo's Urban Renewal Authority, and six other Pueblo civic power brokers, the interview appeared to be a little more intimidating than I had initially anticipated.

I graciously shook hands with all nine inquisitors and they invited me to take a seat at the head of the conference room table. As I stared down at the nine strange faces, they stared back at me. The table was nearly filled to capacity, the person sitting at the other end of it felt like a stones throw away, as if I would have to holler just for her to hear me.

"Mike, why are you interested in this position?" the City Manager asked.

"Well, ya see," I answered, "there's a big difference between 'administrative' and 'policy' decisions . . ."

And so it went.

An hour and a few quarts of sweat later, I walked out of the City Manager's conference room feeling as if I adequately talked myself up. I called my wife during the two and a half hour ride home and explained how I thought the interview went well. Caitlin was pleased.

With my mind bent on the closet campaigning for those on the pro-Tedesco ticket, and my leisurely time spent submitting applications to even the most farfetched jobs, it appeared that, one way or another, my time in La Blanca Gente was beginning to come to a head.

In the meantime, however, there was no immediate change to my lot in life; the cross that I bear remained the same weight.

Days passed. Bitterness rose.

"Are you the Planning Director?" the old man asked from the doorway into my office.

"Indeed I am. Come on in."

We chatted about the snowy weather; then he got to the point. "It appears as if my garage is three feet within the side set-back. I was told by the building inspector that it is illegal and may need to be torn down."

"Wow," I said. "That sounds like some pretty drastic measures for a pretty simple problem to resolve."

"What can we do?" the old man asked. "I would sure hate to demolish my garage over a three-foot misunderstanding."

"We'll have to get you approved for a variance," I responded.

The look of confusion that washed upon the old man's face was unmistakable. "Huh?" he questioned.

"The variance process isn't so bad. Basically what happens is you fill out an application describing your non-conformance with the town's land use code. In this case, your side set-back, and then you go before the Zoning Board of Appeals, who are five people that don't understand the first thing about the town's land use code but hold the fate of your garage in their hands. The good news is, they'll be looking to me for guidance, and I will happily recommend that they approve your variance request. Quite candidly: the Zoning Board of Appeals doesn't know what the hell is going on, so I expect they'll follow my lead. The entire, quite meaningless process takes about 45 days to process and will cost a $200 application fee—just so you can sit before the Council of Zoning Ignorance and watch them stammer about for half an hour before they finally say 'yes.'"

"Nothing like watching our government at work," the old man said with a wink. I gave him the variance application and off he went.

As he left it occurred to me that I didn't even know who sat on the Zoning Board of Appeals, nor did I know the statutory procedures to call a meeting to order. Hearing Ava and Tami chatting from Ava's office, I swallowed hard and accepted the fact that only Ava could help me on this one.

I strolled into her office. "Ava, how does one go about organizing a meeting of the Zoning Board of Appeals?" Before Ava had a chance to respond, Tami intercepted my question. "Can I ask you a question," she said with a tone that signaled trouble. A shot of adrenaline darted through my veins. "What makes you think that it's okay for you to come in here and interrupt our conversation without saying excuse me? You just interrupted our conversation and I think you should have better manners than that."

I glanced over at Ava while Tami was spouting off; she was rubbing her forehead with her eyes closed probably wishing Tami wasn't trying to pick a fight with me.

The air was thick, but I wasn't in the mood to bicker. "Can we bicker later, Tami, I have a headache already. Do you have a minute to give me a hand now, Ava, or do you want to do it later."

But Tami wasn't done. "I'm serious, Mike, I'll either sit here and interrupt the conversation you're trying to have with Ava or you can look me and Ava in the eyes and say 'excuse me for interrupting.'"

I sat silent for a moment, and struggled with an appropriate response. Tami seized her opportunity to pounce. "What's the matter, Mike, you're usually all talk? It must hurt being wrong from time to time? Now how about a Godamn apology?"

"I'm sorry, Tami," I feigned. For a moment, all was silent, and I was the first to break it. "I didn't know that the Manners Police were in Ava's office. I didn't know that I needed to check with Martha Stewart before I approached Ava on work related issues. Additionally, I wasn't aware that your conversation about horses, or whatever the hell it was you two were talking about, takes precedence over work related discussion. But I could be wrong. If you like, princess, I could call the mayor and get his opinion?"

Tami silent. Ava Silent. Already dark and late afternoon, I left Ava's office and went home.

I arrived home that evening to a letter from the City of Pueblo. I opened it slowly, knowing full well what it said—rejection. My heart, once filled with hope, sank as I read the letter and my suspicions were confirmed. Defeated, I looked up at my wife and said, "We're fucked. I didn't get the job."

"Do you have any other leads that you submitted applications to?" was her response.

"No, Pueblo was our last best hope."

Through a bottle of wine and perhaps a cigarette or two, Caitlin and I came to the sad realization that there was nothing left to do but cash in our chips, admit defeat, and look into purchasing a house in the area and sticking with La Blanca Gente for the foreseeable future. The sad reality being that I was still too green to get a planning job worth a damn.

13

Election Day

The day of the election was rapidly approaching. All of my horses appeared to be working diligently to get elected. Phyllis Baine explicitly ran on an anti-Ava/Tami platform, which pleased me and terrified my colleagues in Town Hall. Everything appeared to be going according to plan.

Phyllis walked into my office one morning and closed my door behind her. No one ever closed doors in Town Hall. Ava left her door open, and I mine at all times. Phyllis closing my door behind her was an unprecedented maneuver that surely both stunned and frightened Ava. After a minute of chit-chat, Phyllis got down to business. "Mike, I want to lodge a zoning complaint against Earl Blenni." The statement made me sit back in my office chair. As Phyllis's statement marinated in my head, she decided to add some seasoning to it. "Have you driven by his property lately? I just can't believe the mess. People drive through town and see piles of granite and work materials on his property and it just leaves a bad impression."

Earl, a tradesman who specializes in granite flooring, is also running for the Town Board. A firebrand Texas cowboy who shoots from the hip regardless of what the facts might otherwise dictate. A guy like him really didn't give a damn about the problems at Town Hall; he just wanted looser town regulations so he could run his granite tile business with less government oversight.

"Okay, Phyllis," I said, "Let me grab you a complaint form." I didn't feel good when she left. If Phyllis submits a complaint form prior to the election, then I'll find myself square in the middle of a bickering match between two people who may well be my bosses come election day. I felt bewildered that Phyllis would even want to pick a fight with Earl, much less put me right in the middle of it, particularly this close to the election. Picking a worthwhile fight takes timing and calculus, two elements of Phyllis's decision making process that I fear may be absent from her equation.

The next morning Phyllis again came strutting into my office and delivered a completed land use complaint form. As she left, I held the three page form and caressed the document with a degree of hatred. Nothing like a petty land use complaint to stimulate political activity. It dawned on me that I was a pawn in a game that I knew nothing about. Why would Phyllis, a good friend of mine, subject herself and me to a high risk, low reward situation prior to election day? Why would she pick a fight with a person who may be her colleague on the Town Board? It just didn't add up.

Despite the glaring absence of logic associated with the situation, with the submittal of Phyllis's complaint, I am now bound by La Blanca Gente law to investigate its merits. I knew Earl was not going to appreciate a site visit from me; I knew I would have to draft a memo outlining my findings; and I knew that it was going to be impossible to please both parties once the memo went public. Between Phyllis and Earl, two people that may well be my future bosses, someone was going to be pissed at the results, if not both of them. The following day I made the trip over to Earl's property. Greeted by the hum of heavy machinery, I flagged down Earl and we stepped outside.

"Earl, I received a zoning complaint about this property," I said as I braced myself for his reaction.

"A 'zoning complaint'—what in the hell for?" he responded. Without allowing me to respond, he added a clause to his original statement, "That's exactly what's wrong with this Goddamn town; you people are against a guy trying to run an honest business."

"The complainant is concerned that this property does not conform to the town's land use code." I said.

"Jesus Christ, Mike, I've been on this property for months, and this is the first that anyone's ever said that I can't be doing what I'm doing."

"I'm not saying you can't be doing what your doing, Earl. I'm saying someone's complaining about what your doing, and I'm bound by La Blanca Gente law to investigate."

Earl spent the next few minutes arguing his philosophy regarding private property rights and zoning law.

"Okay, Earl, over the next couple of days, I'm going to draft a memo that outlines whether or not the complaint has merit. In the meantime, why don't you show me around your property?"

After a ten minute tour of Earl's property, I left him to his own small government thinking and returned to my office to compare my notes to the requirements of the land use code. I found myself hoping I would not have to drop the zoning hammer on Earl, who appeared to be a helpless victim. At the same time, however, concern grew as to the best method of handling Phyllis, who sat like a crow atop a perch, at the other end of this complaint.

It took me a couple days to draft the memo, and I vetted it through the town attorney's office. Long story short, I found Earl not to be in violation of the land use code. Phyllis was not going to be pleased. After placing a copy in my files, I mailed a copy to both Earl and Phyllis.

Earl called me the next day. "Mike, what the hell does this memo mean?" Clearly Earl's reading comprehension skills leave something to be desired.

"It means that you're not in violation of the land use code, Earl. You can keep doing what you're doing," I said.

"Why don't you just say that in your letter?"

"I do say that in my letter, Earl, but I have to couch my arguments in terms of the land use code, which is why the letter is a bit more complex than necessary."

"Okay, then, good-bye." Earl hung up.

After a quick stop at my favorite La Blanca Gente liquor store, I drove home from work and, to my shock and amazement, I noticed Phyllis's car parked outside Ava's house. I drove by with my heart in my belly. What the hell was going on? Standing in my kitchen with a bottle opener in one hand and a bottle of IPA in the other, I told Caitlin the news.

"What the hell is going on?" she asked.

"That's what I want to know."

"Aren't we supposed to be friends with them?" Caitlin asked. "She hates Ava. What is she doing at her house?"

"I have no idea, but I sure hope she calls us with the scoop," I said.

The next morning, Phyllis came into Town Hall and, without even saying "hi" to me, went straight into Ava's office and closed the door behind her. I felt both stunned and terrified. My paranoia grew. My mind darted to all the conversations I had with Phyllis regarding all the dirty details and secrets in Town Hall—all the conversations about the Board of Trustees, all the bad mouthing, everything. An hour later, Phyllis reemerged and left Town Hall without acknowledging my presence. Ava cheerily left her office and, with a spring in her step, retired to the kitchen to refresh her coffee.

Caitlin and I became friends with Phyllis and her husband, Tyler, because we enjoyed gossiping about La Blanca Gente together. Phyllis and Tyler also asked some hard questions, mostly on my behalf, at the work session when the Town Board formally defined my job description.

Unfortunately for Caitlin and me, we did not know we made a deal with the devil that night. I had heard many negative things about the Baines from many people, particularly when a given person would ask, "What are you doing tonight?" And I would say, "We're going to have a couple of drinks with the Baines." The response was always the same. "Don't hang out with them, those people are crazy." I never really listened, because everybody talks shit about everybody in La Blanca Gente—it's the number one industry.

As the Tedescos and the Baines were becoming friends, however, I tried not to let Phyllis's eccentricities get to me. Caitlin and I did a good job of giving them the benefit of the doubt and not listening to the nay-sayers. What fools we were.

Irrationally, I convinced Phyllis to run for the Town Board, thinking—hoping—she would make a good person to stand up and tell it like it is. Now, however, with only a few days before election day, it was clear Phyllis betrayed my trust and, worse yet, had now formed an alliance with Ava, my nemesis. Thus, like a game of Go Fish, I had lost one of the three cards in my hand to Ava. Going into election day, we both found ourselves praying a Novena to the Gods of Politics that both of our candidates succeeded—Elroy and Phyllis for Ava, and Jack and Maria for me. Knowing that, historically, the total municipal vote in La Blanca Gente hovers around 100 people, I knew that the election was going to be a horse race.

April 12th, 2006. In the shower that morning I openly prayed to God and asked Him for mercy. Filled with anxiety, I voted right before lunch. Ava, as the Town Clerk, was working the only precinct in La Blanca Gente, so it was my responsibility to man Town Hall all day. The polls closed at 7:00 PM, and I was not sure how long it would take to finalize the vote count. I arrived home at 5:00 to an antsy wife who felt just as eager as I to know the election results. Around 8:00 that evening, Caitlin convinced me to drive to the precinct and see if the polling results were posted.

The precinct, which is the town's community building, was dark as I pulled into the gravel parking area. I got out of my truck to survey the situation. On the window adjacent to the front door I found the booty I was searching for: certified election results.

Too dark to see the dimly lit writing, I pulled out my cigarette lighter to shed some light on the subject. Studying the list with the fervor of a scientist, my nose nearly touching the window, eyes trying to capture the dim light, I felt mixed emotions as I drank in the results: Elroy lost, Maria won, Jack lost, and Phyllis lost.

The good news was Ava no longer had a conduit on the Town Board and, better yet, Elroy was replaced by a pro-Tedesco candidate. The bad news was my other candidate lost. Another newcomer on the Town Board includes a member of the town's Planning and Zoning Commission— Seth Rosenstein. Generally speaking, although I'm sure he's well aware of the personnel problems at Town Hall; his attitude toward the situation was neutral. The third newcomer on the Town Board was Earl Blenni. It remains to be seen if he harbors any negative feelings towards me for processing Phyllis's zoning complaint against him. Therefore, with only three newcomers on the Board of Trustees, the majority opinion, an opinion that tends to favor incompetence above common sense, remains unchanged.

As the distance between election day and my general routine lengthened, I began to wonder when the other shoe was going to drop. Phyllis, now a shameless ally of Ava, attempted to confront me on two different occasions regarding my land use ruling. She even went so far as to secretly record a conversation I had with her in my office regarding the nature of my decision. Thus, with what appeared to be little change as a result of the elections, I pined my time into the usual mindless nonsense.

14

Animosity

---

s April started to press on the month of May, the elections now two weeks behind me, my impatience got the better of me, and I decided to make a push for the town to form a business improvement district. This time, however, I reconfigured my strategy; instead of going to the Town Board to pitch the idea, I decided to pitch the idea to the people who would ultimately support it: the La Blanca Gente Chamber of Commerce.

I talked Dalton into allowing me to address the Chamber members at their regular monthly meeting. Generally speaking, a business improvement district involves circling a given geography of commercial property owners and then they voluntarily levee a property tax on themselves to finance public improvements such as security, marketing, and even some capital improvements like benches and landscaping. The money generated from a district may only be spent within it. The property owners located within a proposed district have to vote on the approval (or disapproval) of the business improvement district. In larger cities, it's fairly routine to have a business improvement district within a downtown or even a neighborhood center.

The challenge that lies before me is to convince the La Blanca Gente business class that there are virtues to raising their own property taxes, that there is virtue in circumventing the Town Board, that there is virtue in taking matters into their own hands.

If they could be convinced to band together and finance their own destiny, the La Blanca Gente Town Board would largely be left out of the decision making equation. Because the revenue generated from the district would go directly to the district's board, the seven Town of La Blanca Gente Trustees would have trouble obstructing the decision making process. With the Town Board out of the way, and with people whose livelihoods depend on quick and decisive action, a business improvement district is a good avenue to neutralize those that tend to get in the way of good planning. Likewise, it would provide the revenue necessary for much needed highway corridor pedestrian improvements.

As speeches go, I was well prepared for this one. Rather than surfing the Internet in my spare office time, I devoted such energy to drafting a five page report outlining the ins and outs of a business improvement district. The monthly Chamber meetings attracted most of the business owners in and around La Blanca Gente—a good 75 people. Although I did not know all of them, they for sure knew of me by reputation, whatever that might be. I drafted the report with the intent to disburse a copy to each and every person who attended the meeting. (I even gave one to the waitress who served the event.) Those who knew me well could sense my desperation, my anxiety—like starting the last round of a boxing match already battered and bruised, clearly losing the fight. My last hope was a little reckless abandon, the knockout punch.

The night before the big speech, I found myself throwing darts at my dart board located within the spare bedroom of my home. With much graciousness, I distracted myself in between throws to slurp on a bottle of cabernet. I'd developed a habit of thinking in front of my dart board. Like yoga in the wilderness, chucking darts in my spare bedroom and simultaneously intoxicating myself became therapeutic.

With each throw of a dart and each gulp of cabernet, I slowly felt the anger creep inside me as I tried to strategize about a suitable speech to give to the Chamber of Commerce. The usual pandering dribble wasn't going to cut it. I thought about all the personal discussions with members of the Chamber, all of their gripes about La Blanca Gente, all of the time and fruitless effort I'd put into projects that never materialized, all the bluster and gossip that amounted to nothing more than impotence.

Ironically, as I threw more darts and drank more wine the picture became clearer and clearer: the only way to motivate these people was to get them angry. Remind them of all the bullshit they put up with in La Blanca Gente, of all the incompetence in Town Hall, of all the obstacles between them and true wealth, feed their conspiracy theories and indulge their paranoia. In a sense, my primary tactic was reverse psychology. The difference being, however, I would say nothing that was the reverse of anything.

The morning of the speech, I arrived at the Ty Webb Club ten minutes early to glad-hand those that needed glad-handing, pander to those who needed pandering, and gawk at those who needed to be gawked.

As the lunch meeting got under way, Tami strolled in to participate in the spectacle. Totally unaware that I was on the agenda, she appeared a bit surprised as I strutted up to the podium. I thought it a testament to the many ambiguous facets of my being. Traditionally, the La Blanca Gente Chamber of Commerce was officially Tami's domain, but not today.

"Hello everyone," I said to the crowded venue. "As most of you already know, I'm Mike Tedesco—the Community Development Director for the Town of La Blanca Gente. If you have never shaken my hand, I'm sure with the help of Tami and Ava, you know me by reputation."

I wink at Tami. I draw a breath as I survey the audience. "Last chance to back out?" I thought to myself.

"But I have nothing to lose because I really haven't gained anything to begin with?" was the response to myself. "Nearly a year of work entangled by pettiness and stupidity adds up to little more than a pot to piss in."

As I debated with myself, a sense of discomfort fell over the crowd as anxiety grew due to the elongated silence. My eyes spot Grady Ryan in the audience. He smiles. A twinkle glimmered in my eye as a big, Tom Cruise smile appeared on my face to return Grady's favor.

"Fuck it."

"I'm tired," I began. "I'm tired of the constant shit talking, the petty belittling, the confounding incompetence, and the stifling ignorance marinated with a touch of paranoia that is the Town of La Blanca Gente."

The faces in the crowd grew dim. For sure, this is not the type of speech that they were expecting. Grady, however, kept smiling. "I've been talking for almost a year about how to turn La Blanca Gente into a true Colorado resort destination and I have been met with nothing more than what I just described. You, the business owners of La Blanca Gente, are my last best hope."

I held up the five page Business Improvement District Report that was handed out prior to the meeting. "Do you know what this is? This is a document that will take you to the Promise Land!" My confidence elicited a couple of random chuckles.

"This is a document that will enable the business owners of La Blanca Gente to control their own destinies. It will enable you to make decisions independent of the La Blanca Gente Town Board and invest public money into pedestrian oriented improvements along the highways—money that can be spent to build sidewalks and street trees, fountains and bike lanes, public art and landscaping. Implementing this document represents the first big step toward taking a seat at the big boys' table of Colorado mountain resort destinations. If you want to compete with the big boys, you need to know how to play the game, and this document will shepherd you through the process of transitioning from sleepy La Blanca Gente to a bustling orgy of shoppers and tourists.

"There are those in town that are so engulfed in their own world of illusion that they think the mountains and trees will disappear if La Blanca Gente 'develops into another Colorado resort town'—they trivialize the term as if it were a bad thing."

I look over at Tami and continue. "These are your enemies. These are the people who wish not to change the status quo. Worse yet, they wish to nurture the status quo, to caress it, and they stroke the absurdity of their philosophy in the absence of reason. In the absence of reason, there is only ignorance. Their ignorance is like a cancer that is fed by gossip, and metastasizes at any suggestion of change. 'Change' in La Blanca Gente is a four-letter word, a temptation from the anti-Christ, like the devil offering Jesus bread and water in the desert. Unlike Jesus in the desert, however, La Blanca Gente is faithless. For faith can't cure ignorance and faith won't raise your profit margins. Perhaps planners are the anti-Christ, but I'm offering you the temptation of change.

"Give in to temptation.

"Not only does it feel good, but you'll find that once you do it the first time subsequent moments of clarity will not be accompanied by such a large degree of guilt. As the town's planner, I am the change agent, the anti-Christ, the stranger offering you candy, the photographer asking you to take off your shirt. My salary being funded by your sales tax dollars, I'm whatever you want me to be—you are my pimp and I your whore, and large returns await those with sack enough to cut me loose.

"You know as well as I do that there are a lot of complainers in this town. The complainers rule this town, but what the complainers do not do is make any suggestions regarding how to fix the problems that they're complaining about. They assail you with a constant barrage of incompetence and ignorance—two negatives that do not make a positive. La Blanca Gente is so far outside the orbit of normal that we have managed to defy the laws of mathematics. For mathematic principles and business knowledge were cast aside long ago for the sake of a closed-minded, obstructionary thought process that gives weight to speculation rather than facts in the range of factors that produce the decision making equation.

"Like you, I've been in this town long enough to know what works and what doesn't. We all know that there's a lot in this town that does not work, and little that does. We're all aware of the problems, what a business improvement district allows you to do is stop complaining and start taking action. It is not a decision subject to approval from the Town Board. The decision is subject to your approval.

"Who are the complainers? Some are in this room, many are in Town Hall, and most are those long-time residents who know little of the world outside the San Luis Valley.

"We all know that the Town of La Blanca Gente operates on pennies and, even if they had extra money, chances are the Town Board would not spend it on what you, as the business owners of La Blanca Gente, need to succeed. Do you really want to stake your future on the back of the Town Board? To me, and I had to learn this the hard way, that is a high-risk, low reward scenario. But that's okay because Dr. Tedesco has a cure for what ails you: raise your own capital via a business improvement district. It's your money, so you call the shots. The beauty being you cut the cancer of incompetence and ignorance out of the decision making equation.

"I'm tired of the constant shit talking, the petty belittling, the confounding incompetence, and the stifling ignorance marinated with a touch of paranoia that is the Town of La Blanca Gente. I'm tired of the madness.

"Residents of the Town of La Blanca Gente have gang-raped reasonability and common sense, and I'm here to take my virginity back."

I stop, look around the room. The crowd looking at me like I just shot Kennedy. The microphone leaves my fingers and lands with a thud onto the podium, and then I strut through the crowded tables and chairs into the lounge that abuts the banquet room and ordered an IPA. There was no applause, just a room full of dumbfounded business owners.

The last thing I hear as I take my beer outside to introduce it to nicotine was Dalton on the microphone stating, "Well, Tedesco certainly gave us all something to think about."

15

Fortuna's Wheel

Towns are a reflection of three primary factors: citizens, elected officials, and town administrators. To be a great place, all three factors need to mesh into a cohesive whole. A difficult task, to say the least. The best urban planners are known for finding a way to bring each group to the table and empower them to feel that their contributions will, in the end, make a difference. Naturally, elected officials already feel empowered. Citizens, however, need some convincing to take a seat at the table. Town administrators, depending on their ambition, can either be cooperative or hesitant in the planning process.

The state of La Blanca Gente reflects past and present dysfunction between the factors necessary to make an urban place succeed. Over the past eleven months, I've been beat down to a nub by a combination of incompetence, closed mindedness, fear, and even hatred. The filth, shameless and brazen as it might be, that is regurgitated from institutionalized town administrators that know oh so little about the world outside of the San Luis Valley and even less about what it takes to stimulate an urban environment, is a burden that I cannot overcome. It smothers me, my ambition, my patience, my open mindedness, my creativity, like a pillow to the face.

I'm only a year out of graduate school and, evidently, that doesn't account for shit in the planning labor market. There are no promising job prospects on the horizon. I'm stuck on a treadmill, forced to face an unpleasant reality that La Blanca Gente will be my home for the foreseeable future and that Ava and Tami will continue to win battles despite their superior capability to exercise stupidity.

Ava and Tami see me as an inept, snobby kid. I've come to realize that, yes, I am quite the snob. I've also come to realize that one shouldn't be ashamed of their snobbery, if practiced in the right manner. To me snobbery is the indulgence in satisfying basic human instincts. A good meal with good wine polished off with good tobacco and, hopefully, shared with good company. That's pretty much all I want out of life, that and to live in a well planned urban environment. I never thought I was a snob before I entered the 3rd dimension of La Blanca Gente. Snobs expect nothing but the best, and there is nothing wrong with that. In fact, if more people were to expect nothing but the best, than perhaps more people would provide their best. I'm no freakin' philosopher, but the problem with La Blanca Gente is not a function of the fact that the town is run by fools. It's a function of the fact that they don't expect the best; they've grown accustomed to "C" quality goods and services and have been conditioned to think that somehow it's okay to accept them. Well, mediocre is not okay with me, and I'm not going to accept it. If that makes me a snob, so be it. And so it goes, La Blanca Gente is my lot in life, the cross that I bear.

Unable to afford a house in the La Blanca Gente market, Caitlin and I are forced to look in Monte Vista, a short drive from La Blanca Gente, on the San Luis Valley floor. We shopped around for a couple of weeks and found a nice little place. We roped in Truett Tilman to act as our real estate agent.

Now early May, the days are noticeably warmer, and the cottonwoods along the Rio Grande are starting to develop a shade of green. As if admitting defeat, I openly chatted with Ava about the house I was about to purchase.

Due to close on Monday, it's now Friday morning and I'm in my office pining away the time surfing the Internet. As I step outside for my customary 10:00 AM cigarette, my cell phone rings. "Hello, is this Mike Tedesco?" queried the voice on the other end.

"Yes it is," I answered.

"Hi Mike, this is Nick Howser with the City of Pueblo Human Resources Department."

A shot of adrenaline pumped through my veins.

"Is now a good time to talk?" Nick asked.

"Sure," was my response.

"Mike, I'm calling to offer you the job of Executive Director for the Urban Renewal Authority of Pueblo. Are you still interested?"

"Are you serious? I got the rejection letter a couple of weeks ago. What's changed?"

"Well," Nick said, "the first offer fell through, and I've been authorized to make you an offer."

"I'll take it. When do I start?"

Nick and I finished our conversation. I hung up and lit another cigarette as I furiously dialed my wife's number to share the news. Caitlin was pleased.

Ava must have wondered what I was doing as I spent the next 45 minutes outside making phone calls, number one on the list being to Truett to cancel the offer on the house that I was only three days away from purchasing.

I walked back into Town Hall ready—almost hoping—Ava would pop an attitude with me so I could unleash almost a year's worth of frustration. For the rest of the day, I sat in my office and fantasized about the things I would say if only Ava could cross the line one more time. I was praying for a fight, an opportunity for me, now that I finally had nothing to lose, to open the floodgates. I needed a cleansing, a therapeutic moment.

After nearly a year's worth of pure, unadulterated insanity, I intentionally kept everyone in Town Hall from knowing that I was only a few days away from submitting my two-week notice. I lurked around like a lion in the grass, just waiting for the best opportunity to pounce. Just one more chance, just one more phone call between Ava and Elroy clearly talking negatively about me, just one more incomprehensionable moment between me and Tami.

Unfortunately, the Almighty displayed His mercy on Ava and Tami—one last fight was not to be. I've always been good at picking a fight. Either out of principle or just to experience the theatre of it. My challenge has always been, however, winning the fights that I pick. I've gotten my ass kicked enough times, either metaphorically or literally, to know that perhaps I should be a bit more selective when instigating conflict.

Graduate school can prepare no man to surmount such hurdles, incompetence that is. Graduate school teaches nothing of politics, or how to communicate. It's all theoretical. It's easy to conjure up virtuous planning while sitting in an ivory tower, but the rules of engagement are much different when you're in the trenches fighting for even the table scraps of "good planning." Institutions move slowly, they resist change, and La Blanca Gente's Town Clerk is no exception. One of the gaping holes in graduate studies is a distinct void of any type of discussion relevant to municipal politics. No one ever told my classmates or I that "change" is a four letter word. That, despite what you've learned in graduate school, you really won't know shit once you hit the labor market. All the books you've read, all the boring-ass journal articles that you had to stomach, all the Godamn papers you wrote amount to surprising little credibility for practicing planners.

To make matters worse, The American Planning Association (APA) pushes their AICP certification like to take the exam is to take a drink from the Holy Grail. The APA implies that the planning master's degree you just dropped $40,000 and two years of bloodshed to earn is actually quite worthless. Planners can thank the APA for the diminished credibility of a master's degree and, considering their fetish with finding ways to better write and institute government regulations, the diminished credibility of the field as a whole. Needless to say, I've let my membership lapse. Urban Land Institute, here I come.

La Blanca Gente needs an easy win, something to hang their hat on. It's like collegiate football. All the teams that are in the national title hunt year after year pad their schedules with, what are considered, powder-puff victories in an effort to maintain their high national rankings prior to playing their conference schedule. La Blanca Gente is the latent national power house that needs to play a couple of junior college teams to build some confidence.

When the La Blanca Gente Music Association was lobbying the Town Board to place a band-shell on town property—property adjacent to the golden waters of the Rio Grande—they got talked out of it in an effort to build on a parcel managed by the Bureau of Land Management. A clearly superior site, but an effort that would literally take an act of congress to make happen. Only inches away from gaining approval for using a town site, with volunteer labor lined up and ready to improve the site and start construction, the idea of using a vacant, town, three acre parcel adjacent to the Rio Grande River was abandoned. Folly, indeed, because it would have been a tangible change in the community that people could point to with pride, that would have laid the seeds of an annual music festival, that could have put the nay-sayers in their place. When the suggestion was pitched that the band-shell ought to be moved to the Bureau of Land Management site, I just did not have the sack to tell everyone that I disagreed with their decision. By virtue of the politics of the situation, I had failed. Now, the band-shell still is not built, and the La Blanca Gente Music Association is pointed to by Ava and her ilk as just another passing fad, a fad that came and went (just like every other fad), a fad that had no materiel effect on the community, and is no longer a factor in the discourse of La Blanca Gente politics.

Wolf Creek still looms on the horizon—cited by nearly everyone as inevitable but always just a step away from starting construction. The environmental forces opposing the project managed to gain a court decreed injunction in October of 2007, which put a hold on the project on the grounds that ". . . questions going to the merits [of the Village project] are so serious, substantial, difficult, and doubtful as to make the issue ripe for litigation and deserving of more deliberate investigation."[45] The money driving the Village at Wolf Creek finally figured out that their front man, Billy Jacto, just isn't getting the job done. Billy was replaced by Dan Johnson—Vice President of Texas-based Dan Johnson Development. I think I speak for all in the San Luis Valley that a little more compromise and a little less Texas snake oil salesman would go a long way. At this point, the project is being pushed by ego rather than common sense and, as a result, the Village at Wolf Creek is still only a phantom of the imagination. The La Blanca Gente Chamber of Commerce alongside the San Luis Valley Economic Development Council fudged their moment of opportunity to gain credibility as reasonable liaisons to broker a deal between the forces for and against the Village Project. Now, they're just seen as the only people who have taken a drink of the Kool-Aid. Pushing a drug that no one wants, both local entities would do well to take steps to re-gain their lost credibility.

As for those who are responsible for shepherding the project through the Federal environmental impact process, i.e., the US Forest Service, credibility appears to be in short supply there, too. On Thursday, February 17, 2009, the team tagged with the responsibility to oversee the Federal regulatory process was sacked. That same week, a Forest Service public affairs official lamented, "Bottom line for us is we don't have the capacity to work such a big project with our own people."[46] In the mean time, the development team was told to throw away the second version of their environmental impact statement due to development plan changes that were decided at a local level, i.e., Jamie Welsh's office in Creede.

Indeed, the more the residents of La Blanca Gente try, the more opportunity slips through their fingers. The town lumbers along like a three-legged dog. They just can't help but screw things up. Even Garrett Cook, La Blanca Gente's Chief of Police, and a man without the absence of integrity, managed to fumble away his job. Garrett's blood flows more pure than the headwaters of the Rio Grande. He doesn't drink, doesn't smoke, doesn't take drugs, and he doesn't drink caffeine. Garrett, at least during the time that I knew him, was a man that operated on principle, a man that had a clear line and he would be polite until you crossed it. Little punks like me don't screw with guys like Garrett Cook. You just say "hi" in the hallway, perhaps mention the weather, and then be on your way.

Garrett resigned as the Town of La Blanca Gente Chief of Police in January of 2008. Several months earlier, according to the local paper, "The town [Board of Trustees] announced that there is an internal investigation going on within the police department regarding an undisclosed incident."[47] A testament to the state of La Blanca Gente journalism, it appears the only person in La Blanca Gente that does not know what happened is the reporter attempting to cover the story.

Gossip is La Blanca Gente's number one industry and it appears that Garrett, one of his deputies, and a La Blanca Gente Trustee broke into a local business and ransacked an office. Motive is unknown. It is also unknown if Garrett was there to stop them or to help them. Either way, Garrett was implicated in the investigation and resigned as a result, regardless of his guilt or innocence. Survival of the fittest, indeed, and Garrett just got cornered by the hyenas.

You will also be happy to know that the carping culture is alive and well in La Blanca Gente. On the November, 2007, municipal ballot, the Board of Trustees placed a question requesting property owners within La Blanca Gente pay an additional three mills in property taxes to finance street improvements, upkeep, and maintenance. Translated in monetary terms, this would have increased the property taxes on your typical

$500,000 mountain cabin by roughly $119 annually. The ballot question failed with a resounding "NO."

True to La Blanca Gente form, about three months later during public comment at a meeting of the Board of Trustees, Floyd Gannio managed to prove the hypocrisy of the La Blanca Gente voting public by complaining about the lack of snow removal from the streets in his neighborhood.[48]

And thus is La Blanca Gente, perhaps the only place on Earth where residents will vote down the funding for street maintenance and then have the audacity to complain about the lack of street maintenance only a few months later.

It's much better being a spectator than a participator. Only a couple of hours from La Blanca Gente, on the low-lands of the Front Range, I watch from my nest in Pueblo and smirk to myself as La Blanca Gente continues along the path of incompetence. The collective personality of the town is like that of a toddler who covers his ears and closes his eyes whenever someone suggests something new.

How could I have done things differently? More importantly, how can planners actually accomplish "good planning?" Much of my failures during my tenure in La Blanca Gente rest more on my shoulders than on those who worked against me. All other things being equal, the planners who get things done are the planners who exercise patience, modesty, and good politicking—three aspects of my professional life that were absent during my time in La Blanca Gente.

Despite a degree of hostility left on both sides, vacating La Blanca Gente was the best option for both parties. Without a doubt, it's best to let the locals screw up their own town. They don't need my help doing it.

Notes

1

Networking

[1] American Planning Association. "Information for the AICP Comprehensive Planning Examination." Web Resource. Accessed March, 15, 2009. www.planning.org/certification/pdf/bulletin.pdf

[2] American Planning Association. "PlanningBooks.com." Web Resource. Accessed March 15, 2009. www.myapa.planning.org/APAStore/Search/Default.aspx?p=3943

[3] American Planning Association. "APA Member Dues." Web Resource. Accessed March 15, 2009. www.planning.org/join/dues/index.htm

[4] American Planning Association. "What is Certification Maintenance?" Web Resource. Accessed March 15, 2009. www.planning.org/cm/whatiscm.htm

2

Aloha Means Goodbye

[5] Duncan, Dayton. *Miles from Nowhere: Tales from the Contemporary Frontier.* First Bison Books. 2000. Page 99.

3

Shelob

[6] Sinclair, Upton. *The Jungle.* Barnes and Noble Books. 2005. Page 36.

[7] Burke, Barlow. *Understanding the Law of Zoning and Land Use Controls.* Mathew Bender and Company. 2002.

[8] Ibid.

[9] Frank, Thomas. *What's the Matter with Kansas.* Metropolitan Books. 2004. Page 43.

[10] Garreau, Joel. *Edge Cities.* First Anchor Books. 1992. Page 185.

[11] Rousseau, Jean-Jacques. *Discourse on the Origin of Inequality.* [1755]. Translated by Franklin Philip. Oxford University Press. 1994.

[12] Ibid

[13] Bromley, Daniel W. "Rousseau's Revenge: The Demise of the Freehold Estate." Ed. Jacobs, Harvey M. *Who Owns America: Social Conflict over Property Rights.* University of Wisconsin Press. 1998.

[14] Ibid

[15] Reps, John W. "Requiem for Zoning." Pomeroy Memorial Lecture. 1964.

4

Planning Incompetence

[16] Colorado Department of Transportation. "About CDOT." Web Resource. Accessed November 12, 2007. www.dot.state.co.us/TopContent/AboutCDOT.asp

[17] Jacobs, Allan. *Great Streets.* MIT Press. 1995. Page 312.

[18] Ibid.

[19] Andres Duany, Elizabeth Plater-Zyberk, and Jeff Speck. *Suburban Nation: the Rise of Sprawl and the Decline of the American Dream.* North Point Press. 2000. Page xi.

[20] [Town of La Blanca Gente], Colorado. "Land Use and Development Code." Adopted November 10th, 2005.

[21] Jacobs, Jane. *The Death and Life of Great American Cities.* Vintage Books. 1992. Page 147.

[22] Smart Growth Network. *Getting to Smart Growth II.* International City/County Management Association (ICMA). 2004.

[23] Ibid.

[24] Rudzitis, Gundars. *Wilderness and the Changing American West.* John Wiley and Sons. 1996. Page 135.

6
Marketing Incompetence

[25] Hall, Peter. *Cities of Tomorrow*. Blackwell Publishing. 2002. Page 193.
[26] Kunstler, James Howard. *The City in Mind*. The Free Press. 2001. Page 67.
[27] Ibid.
[28] Rybczinski, Witold. *City Life*. Scribner. 1995. Page 140.
[29] Hall, Peter. *Cities of Tomorrow*. Blackwell Publishing. 2002. Page 189.
[30] Andres Duany, Elizabeth Plater-Zyberk, and Jeff Speck. *Suburban Nation: the Rise of Sprawl and the Decline of the American Dream*. North Point Press. 2000. Page 10.
[31] Coupland, Douglas. *Generation X: Tales for an Accelerated Culture*. St. Martin's Press. 1991. Page 171.

7
Show Me the Money

[32] Mike E. Miles, Gayle Berens, and Marc A. Weiss. *Real Estate Development: Principles and Process*. Urban Land Institute. Third Edition. 2003. Page 212.
[33] Tedesco, Mike. "Commercial Market Analysis." [Town of La Blanca Gente], Colorado. 2006. Page 17.
[34] International Council of Shopping Centers, National Association of Counties, and the Metropolitan Institute of Virginia Tech. *Developing Successful Retail in Developing and Secondary Markets*. International Council of Shopping Centers. 2007. Page 7.
[35] Developing Neighborhood Alternatives Project. "The Right Tool for the Job? An Analysis of Tax Increment Financing." *Policy Studies*. The Heartland Institute. March, 2003. Page 2.
[36] Department of Community Development. "City Wide TIF Map." City of Chicago. Web Resource. Accessed February 19, 2009. www.egov.cityofchicago.org
[37] Developing Neighborhood Alternatives Project. "The Right Tool for the Job? An Analysis of Tax Increment Financing." *Policy Studies*. The Heartland Institute. March, 2003. pg 6.
[38] Ibid.

11
The Village at Wolf Creek

[39] Garreau, Joel. *The Nine Nations of North America.* Houghton Mifflin Company. 1981.

[40] Ibid.

[41] Rudzitis, Gundars. *Wilderness and the Changing American West.* John Wiley and Sons. 1996. Page 127.

[42] Egan, Timothy. *Lasso the Wind.* Vintage Books. 1998. Page 6.

[43] Colorado House of Representatives. "Legislators to Boycott April 7 Forum in Creede." *State Capital.* Denver, Colorado. April 4, 2006.

[44] Smith, Erin. "Village at Wolf Creek forum draws protestors, developers." *The Pueblo Chieftain.* Pueblo, Colorado. Published April 9th, 2006.

15
Fortuna's Wheel

[45] Judge John L. Kane. "Colorado Wild Inc. and San Luis Valley Ecosystem Council vs. United States Forest Service and [Buckley Hasslbeck] Joint Venture." Filed 10/04/2007.

[46] Hildner, Matt. "Forest Service scraps Wolf Creek team." *The Pueblo Chieftain.* Pueblo, Colorado. Published February 14, 2009.

[47] James, Robin. "Interim Chief Conducts Internal Investigation" [*The La Blanca Gente Local Newspaper.*] August 27, 2007. Web Resource.

[48] James, Robin. "Town Hears Former Police Officer, Citizen Comments." [*The La Blanca Gente Local Newspaper.*] January 18th, 2008. Web Resource.

CPSIA information can be obtained at www.ICGtesting.com
Printed in the USA
LVOW13s1453221213

366444LV00003B/443/P